USAF

PLANS AND POLICIES

IN SOUTH VIETNAM

1961 - 1963

(U)

by

Jacob Van Staaveren

USAF Historical Division Liaison Office

June 1965

Published by Books Express Publishing
Copyright © Books Express, 2012
ISBN 978-1-78039-648-4

Books Express publications are available from all good retail and online booksellers. For publishing proposals and direct ordering please contact us at: info@books-express.com

FOREWORD

USAF Plans and Policies in South Vietnam, 1961-1963, follows two previous studies prepared on counterinsurgency by the USAF Historical Division Liaison Office: USAF Counterinsurgency Doctrines and Capabilities, 1961-1962, and USAF Special Air Warfare Doctrines and Capabilities, 1963.

This study outlines the role of Headquarters USAF in aiding the South Vietnamese effort to defeat the communist-led Viet Cong. The author begins by discussing general U.S. policy leading to increased military and economic assistance to South Vietnam. He then describes the principal USAF deployments and augmentations, Air Force efforts to obtain a larger military planning role, some facets of plans and operations, the Air Force-Army divergencies over the use and control of airpower in combat training and in testing, defoliation activities, and USAF support for the Vietnamese Air Force. The study ends with an account of events leading to the overthrow of the Diem government in Saigon late in 1963.

Because this study emphasizes plans and policies, no effort has been made to chronicle the hundreds of individual air actions in which USAF units participated. However, operational data for the 1961-1963 period is available in the appendices and in other sources, including histories of the participating commands and units, some of which are on file in the USAF Historical Division Liaison Office.

MAX ROSENBERG
Chief
USAF Historical Division
 Liaison Office

CONTENTS

FOREWORD

I. EARLY PLANNING 1
    Background 2
    The Counterinsurgency Plan 5
    The Program of Action 7
    The Taylor Mission 9

II. STEPPING UP MILITARY ASSISTANCE 14
    Establishment of USMAC/V 14
    Establishment of 2d ADVON 17
    Deployment of USAF Aircraft 18
    Deployment of Support Equipment 19

III. PLANS AND OPERATIONS (December 1961-June 1962) 22
    Operational Planning 22
    USAF Operations and Augmentations 23
    The Interdiction Issue 26

IV. PLANS AND OPERATIONS (July 1962-December 1963) 29
    Planning For An Early Victory 29
    USAF Augmentation 32
    USAF/VNAF Operations 34

V. THE DISPUTE OVER AIRPOWER 39
    The JCS Review 39
    The Interdiction Issue Again 42
    The Problem of Army Aviation 43
    Problems of Command Relations 46

VI. TESTING CONCEPTS AND WEAPONS 49
    Supervision of Testing 49
    Test Results 53
    Defoliation 56

VII. USAF SUPPORT OF THE VIETNAMESE AIR FORCE 62
    A Vietnamese Army Air Force? 62
    Buildup of the VNAF 63
    The Problem of Jet Aircraft 66

VIII. THE OVERTHROW OF THE DIEM GOVERNMENT 69
    Conflicting Evaluations of the War 69
    The Fall of the Diem Regime 72
    The "Number One" Problem 74

IX. SUMMARY, 1961-1963 76

NOTES 81
GLOSSARY 97
APPENDICES: STATISTICS ON SOUTH VIETNAM 99
    Appendix 1 - Farmgate Combat Training Sorties 100
    Appendix 2 - Results of Farmgate Missions 101
    Appendix 3 - USAF U-10 and TO-1D Sorties 101
    Appendix 4 - USAF C-123 and SC-47 Sorties and Logistic
                  Activities. 102
    Appendix 5 - VNAF A-1H and T-28 Sorties 103
    Appendix 6 - U.S. and VNAF Military Aircraft 104
    Appendix 7 - U.S. Aircraft Lost, 1 Jan 1962-31 Mar 1964 . . . 104
    Appendix 8 - USAF Aircraft Destroyed and Damaged 105
    Appendix 9 - U.S. Military Personnel. 105
    Appendix 10 - Combat Casualties 106

MAPS AND CHARTS

    1. Vietnam . . . . Frontispiece

                                                      Facing Page

    2. Corps Areas and Primary Airfields in South Vietnam . . . 46
    3. U.S. Military Assistance Command, Vietnam 47

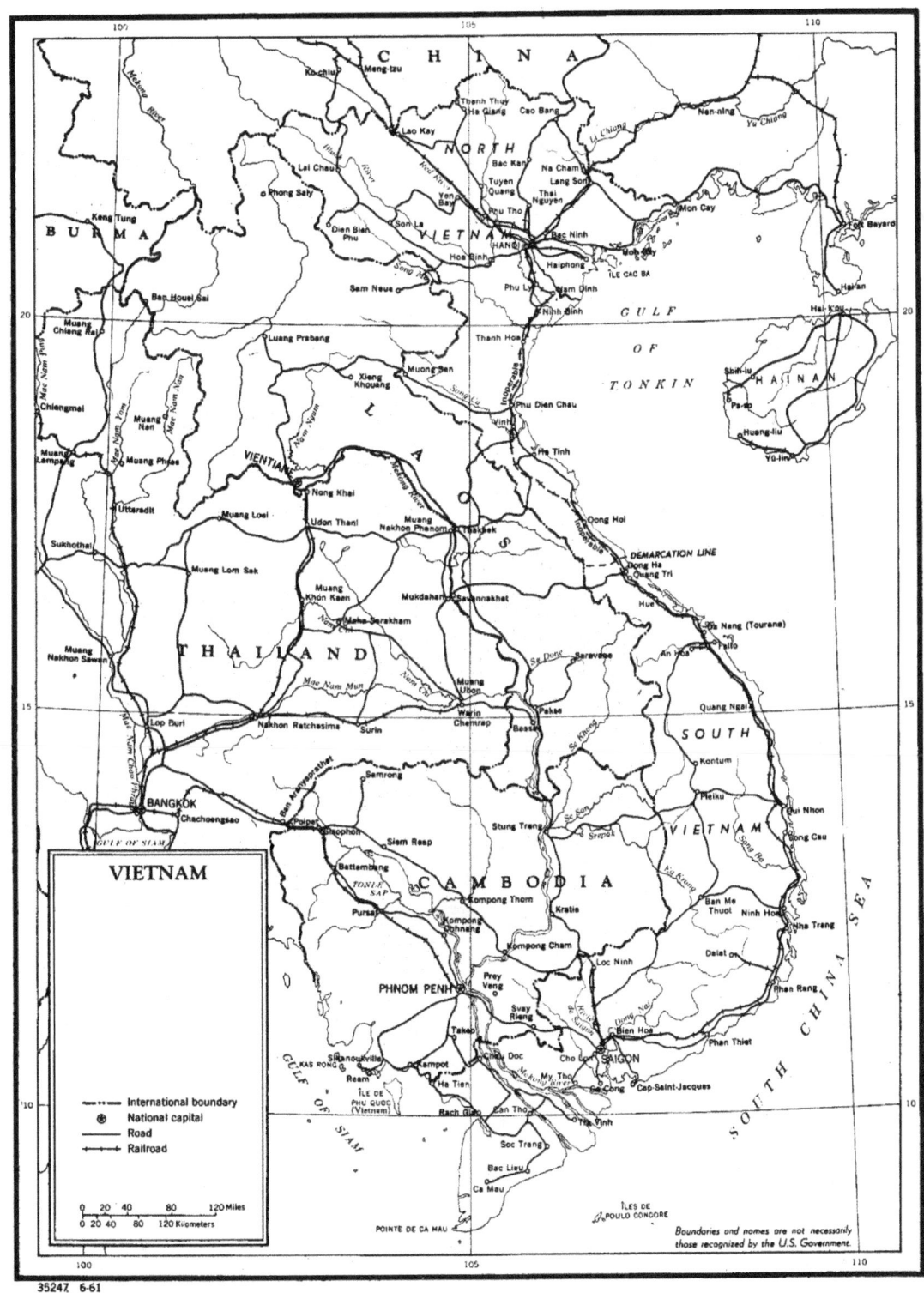

I. EARLY PLANNING

On 7 May 1954 the fortress at Dien Bien Phu surrendered to the Communist-dominated Viet Minh,* signaling the end of the rule of the French in Indochina that had begun in 1862. At a conference held in Geneva, Switzerland, between 26 April and 21 July 1954, France agreed to the "full independence and sovereignty" of Vietnam, Laos, and Cambodia, new nations which evolved out of Indochina. Vietnam would be divided along the 17th parallel of latitude, with the French forces withdrawing south of that line, the Viet Minh north. Separate administrations on each side would consult in July 1955 on "free and general elections by secret ballot" in June 1956 to unify the country. The newly created International Control Commission for Supervision and Control, made up of representatives of India, Canada, and Poland, would supervise the truce arrangements.[1]

Neither the government south of the 17th parallel nor the United States signed the Geneva agreement. Under Secretary of State Walter B. Smith asserted, however, that the United States would not use force to disturb the agreement, that it would view violation as a serious threat to international peace and security, and that it would continue to seek unity through free elections supervised by the United Nations.[2]

---

*The Viet Minh (Vietnam Independence League), founded in May 1941, was a coalition of 16 revolutionary groups which had as a common objective the abolition of French and Japanese rule in Vietnam. After World War II the Viet Minh gradually set up a Communist-controlled regime in North Vietnam which after the Geneva agreement became "The Democratic People's Republic of Vietnam."

Meanwhile, South Vietnam prepared for nationhood. In July 1954 Ngo Dinh Diem became prime minister, and on 26 October 1955, following a referendum, president. On the same day he proclaimed the establishment of The Republic of Vietnam. In 1955, on the grounds that North Vietnam was violating the Geneva agreement and would not allow free elections and that his own country had not signed the agreement, Diem refused to undertake negotiations to unify the country.[3]

Background

The legacy of war found South Vietnam in political, economic, and social chaos. At the end of hostilities in 1954 its population of about 12.5 million (compared with 14 million in North Vietnam) increased by about 900,000 when refugees, largely Catholic, fled the Communist sector. Thousands of Communist guerrillas roamed the countryside, and private armies added to the disorder. And the lack of leadership, free of the taint of French or Viet Minh collaboration, exacerbated the nation's difficulties.[4]

To control unruly elements, the Diem government inherited from the French the Army of the Republic of Vietnam (ARVN)--some 250,000 men. Since the French had occupied the high command positions, the army had virtually no qualified Vietnamese for staff officers. It was also woefully weak in artillery, heavy armor, engineering, and communications. Not until 1955 was the government able to assume effective administrative responsibility for the army.[5]

The Republic of Vietnam Air Force (VNAF), also inherited from the French, had been organized in 1950 as an arm of the army to aid the

French Air Force in the battle for Indochina. Until 1954, when it received its first combat aircraft, the VNAF flew only liaison and observation missions. Some of its aircraft were French, but most were obtained under the United States military assistance program.[6]

The outbreak of the Korean War prompted the U.S. government to send a military assistance advisory group (MAAG/V) to Saigon in July 1950, and on 23 December of that year the United States signed a mutual defense assistance agreement with France and Vietnam. In September 1954 the United States and six other nations signed the Southeast Asia Treaty Organization (SEATO) pact which included a pledge of military assistance, if requested, to South Vietnam. On 1 January 1955 the United States agreed to send military assistance directly to South Vietnam and to assist in organizing and training its armed forces under the overall authority of the commander of the French forces remaining in the country.[7]

The United States briefly shared with the French the task of training and equipping the South Vietnamese military forces. At the request of the South Vietnamese government, the French withdrew their mission for the army in April 1956 and for the air force in May 1957. At this point the United States became solely responsible for advising and supporting the Vietnamese armed forces.[8]

With U.S. financial support, South Vietnam reduced its armed forces to 150,000 men and stepped up it training program.* In 1956 the air force became a separate arm of the Department of National Defense and in May 1957 it possessed four squadrons: one F8F, one C-47, and two L-19 for a total of 85 aircraft. None were combat ready. Authorized personnel strength was 4,000; the number assigned, 4,115. In fiscal year 1958, the VNAF was authorized 4,580, and shortly afterwards it had six squadrons.[9]

As the Diem government continued to manifest greater military, political, and economic viability, the North Vietnamese decided in May 1959 to reunify the country by force. An insurgent group known as the Viet Cong+ that included about 3,000 armed guerrillas began a campaign of major subversion against South Vietnam. It drew its strength from former Viet Minh members who were ordered to remain underground in the south after the 1954 Geneva agreement, Viet Minh troops from the south who regrouped in the north, and elements of the southern population susceptible to Viet Cong recruitment. The insurgency was facilitated by the use of Laos as both corridor and sanctuary. Confronted with this Communist challenge, the United States in 1960 began to plan

---

*South Vietnam also established a Civil Guard and a Self Defense Force to help control the groups that were spreading disorder. The Civil Guard, initially a paramilitary organization controlled by province chiefs, was later administered by the government's Department of Interior. The 40,000-man Self Defense Force, organized on a village basis with locally recruited personnel but headed by regular Army officers, was attached to the government's Department of National Defense.

+Viet Cong is a derogatory abbreviation used in South Vietnam for "those who direct guerrilla warfare and who are subversive agents," that is, Vietnamese Communists. The term in not used in the north.

for and provide increased military and economic assistance to its embattled ally.[10]

The Counterinsurgency Plan

During 1960 the Viet Cong became a dangerous threat to the established government in South Vietnam. The insurgents fought with arms left behind by the Viet Minh in 1954 or obtained from North Vietnam, and they also captured about 80 percent of the 3,700 weapons lost by the Vietnamese forces in 1960. During the year they not only conducted large, coordinated strikes but also 3,645 small ambushes, and they assassinated or kidnapped 2,647 village and hamlet officials. In the Mekong delta, the Viet Cong eliminated local government control and established a "liberated" area where they forcibly taxed the populace. Early in 1960, South Vietnamese intelligence estimated "hard core" Communist strength at 9,820, sympathizers at 2 million, and those "on the fence" at 2 million. According to this estimate, about one-third of the population either preferred Viet Cong rule or was indifferent to it.[11]

In April 1960, before the extensive growth in insurgency activities, Admiral Harry Felt, Commander-in-Chief, Pacific (CINCPAC) had prepared a plan aimed specifically at combating the Viet Cong. The JCS, after reviewing it, recommended to Secretary of Defense Thomas S. Gates that all U.S. agencies concerned with South Vietnam develop a coordinated plan. After many revisions by American officials in Washington and Saigon, the coordinated plan was ready in January 1961 for final review by a new administration which had promised to give greater attention to all aspects of counterinsurgency.*12

The plan urged measures to remedy some political features of the Diem regime that created discontent. It stressed the need for personal security for the Vietnamese and for military, economic, and political reforms to achieve it. The plan also called for adding 20,000 men to the armed forces, raising their strength to 170,000, and improving the Civil Guard. On 30 January President John F. Kennedy and his Secretary of Defense, Robert S. McNamara, approved the plan and the outlay of $28.4 million for the armed forces and $12.7 million for the Civil Guard. The JCS approved implementation of the plan on 6 February.[13]

Although Headquarters USAF supported augmentation of Vietnamese armed forces, it thought the additional manpower allotted to the struggling VNAF was much too small. The VNAF would receive only 499 more men, 400 of these for AD-6 fighter and H-19 and H-34 helicopter units.[14]

In February 1961 the U.S. Ambassador to South Vietnam, Frederick E. Nolting, Jr., presented the counterinsurgency plan to President Diem. Because many provisions were unpalatable to him, Diem eventually issued only a few directives in support of it. He formed a committee to direct operations, transferred control of the Civil Guard from the Department of Interior to the Department of National Defense, developed plans to clarify authority for unified action under a single chain of command, and created corps and division tactical zones in place of military regions.[15]

---

*For a discussion of this issue, see Charles H. Hildreth, "USAF Counterinsurgency Doctrines and Capabilities, 1961-1962" (AFCHO, February 1964), pp 1-4.

The Program of Action

Increased Communist activity in South Vietnam and Laos prompted U.S. authorities to devise a program of action for the Diem government. Prepared by an interagency task force headed by Deputy Secretary of Defense Roswell L. Gilpatric, the new program incorporated much of the old one but was far broader. At a National Security Council meeting on 29 April 1961, President Kennedy approved numerous measures contained in the program: augmentation of the military assistance advisory group (MAAG/V) in Saigon to help train the expanding Vietnamese forces, shipment of radar surveillance equipment to detect Communist overflights and maintain aerial surveillance on the Laotian border, establishment of a combat development and test center, and expansion of the civic action and economic development programs.[16]

On 11 May the President approved a final draft of the program of action for South Vietnam. It was designed to prevent "communist domination, create a viable and increasingly democratic society, and institute . . . mutually supporting actions. . . of military, economic, psychological, and covert character. . . ." He asked for an assessment of the value and cost of further increasing the armed forces from 170,000 to 200,000 by creating "two new division equivalents" for the northwest border region. The President also directed the Department of Defense to continue its studies of the size and composition of the U.S. forces that might be needed for operations in South Vietnam should a meeting between Vice President Lyndon B. Johnson and President Diem scheduled for 11-13 May indicate such a need. On 13 May a Vietnam-U.S. communique stated, however, that both governments would build up existing programs of military and economic aid and that Vietnam's regular armed forces would be increased with U.S. assistance.[17]

Headquarters USAF strongly supported the program of action, suggesting only minor changes concerning personnel, equipment, and logistics. Previously, it had urged the preparation of this type of document for each area of the world where Communist encroachment existed or was expected. Secretary of the Air Force Eugene M. Zuckert called the program an "outstanding job" and a "realistic basis for /an/ aggressive start in reversing /the/ trend of events in Southeast Asia."[18]

In July and August President Kennedy made several other decisions relating to the program. After receiving JCS and OSD recommendations and the report of a U.S. financial survey group headed by the noted economist, Dr. Eugene Staley, he approved increasing the armed forces to 200,000 men. (In February 1962 they were raised to 205,000.) He made approval contingent on devising a satisfactory strategic plan to control the Viet Cong. The President deferred, however, a decision on Diem's request to raise military strength to 270,000 over a two-year period.[19]

With the Staley report as a guide, President Kennedy authorized more funds to carry out the program of action. He counseled U.S. officials to urge Diem to accept the program's reforms. And he directed that Diem be informed that the U.S. President agreed with the Staley Report's three basic tenets as they applied to the program of action: (1) security requirements should have first priority; (2) military operations could not achieve lasting results unless economic and social programs were continued and accelerated; and (3) it was in the interest of both countries to achieve a free society and a self-sustaining economy in South Vietnam.[20]

The Taylor Mission

These measures came too late. As the military situation worsened in South Vietnam and its neighbors, the JCS urged the deployment of SEATO troops to Laos to save that country and to protect the borders of South Vietnam and Thailand.* But the President decided on alternate actions. On 11 October he authorized U.S. advisors to assist in counter-guerrilla operations against Techepone, Laos, a Viet Cong supply center. And, subject to Diem's concurrence, he authorized the dispatch of a detachment from USAF's Special Air Warfare Center to train the VNAF. Presaging additional U.S. involvement, he also ordered his Military Representative, General Maxwell D. Taylor, to Saigon to explore additional ways for more effective U.S. assistance. On the 24th, in a public letter to Diem, President Kennedy assured him of U.S. determination to help Vietnam preserve its independence.[21]

Composed of White House, State, Defense, and other officials, the Taylor Mission visited Southeast Asia from 15 October to 3 November 1961. In its report to the President, the mission warned that the Communists were pursuing

---

*In May 1962 the United States sent combat troops to Thailand where they remained for several months.

> a clear and systematic strategy in Southeast
> Asia. . . to by-pass U.S. nuclear strength. . .
> rooted in the fact that international law and
> practice does not yet recognize the mounting of
> guerrilla war across borders as aggression,
> justifying counter-attack at the source.

The mission noted that Viet Cong strength had risen from about 14,350 in July 1961 to 16,600 in November. But it also discerned Viet Cong weaknesses--the need to rely on terror and intimidation, reluctance to engage the ARVN openly, and fear of U.S. reaction. The Diem government estimated "positive" supporters of Communism within South Vietnam at 200,000, twice the number calculated by American sources.

The mission found that the Diem regime lacked confidence because of Viet Cong successes and uncertainty concerning U.S. policy in Laos. Because of inadequate intelligence, ground forces were engaged in static tasks. Command channels at both the provincial and national levels were unclear and unresponsive, and Diem's distrust of his military commanders exacerbated this feeling. But his government had certain assets, particularly the Army, Civil Guard, and Self Defense Force. The VNAF was ineffective because it lacked target intelligence and its command structure was incomplete. The Vietnamese Navy potential was not yet established.

The Taylor Mission recommended wide-ranging changes. It called for the U.S. military organization to change its relationship with the Diem government from advice-giving to partnership and to become something approximating an operational headquarters in a theater of war. The Diem regime should be brought closer to the people. There should be more emphasis on border control and additional covert operations in North and South Vietnam and in Laos. The United States should step up training and equipping of Vietnamese ground, air, naval, paramilitary, and special forces, and improve communication and intelligence organizations. It should build up MAAG/V to an 8,000-man force, place more emphasis on research and development, and give fast military and economic support to limited offensive operations. To provide more air support, the mission supported the dispatch of the USAF unit (Farmgate) and proposed the shipment of other aircraft and helicopters. Finally, it saw merit in the proposal of Admiral Felt and Ambassador Nolting that the United States should hasten this aid by immediately delivering units and equipment under the guise of helping the populace in recently flooded areas of the Mekong delta.[22]

The proposals were less forceful than those previously advocated by McNamara and the JCS. Observing that the fall of South Vietnam would lead to fairly rapid communization of neighboring nations, they desired deployment of a strong U.S. military force rather than a gradual entry of units. They proposed warning the North Vietnamese government of punitive action unless Viet Cong activities ceased. If North Vietnam and Communist China intervened, they believed that about 200,000 troops, including reserves, could contain the aggressors. Although the United States faced a grave international situation over Berlin, McNamara and the JCS believed that this action in Vietnam would not seriously interfere with plans to defend the German city.[23]

After OSD consultations with State, in which the JCS did not participate, the two departments issued a milder memorandum in November. Warning of the military escalation that might result if U.S. troops were sent, the memorandum noted other possible dangers: failure because of Vietnamese apathy and hostility, political repercussions in the United States if only U.S. troops were used, and renewed Communist action in Laos that might prevent a political settlement in that country. The memorandum also pointed to advantages in obtaining third-country assistance for South Vietnam.[24]

The President, after discussing the memorandum with the National Security Council, decided against the use of U.S. ground forces and adopted a policy of limited participation similar to that recommended by the Taylor Mission. On 22 November he directed that Diem be informed of our willingness to increase aid in a joint undertaking. The United States would provide more men and equipment, step up training, and help establish better communication and intelligence systems. Diem, in turn, would place South Vietnam on a war footing, mobilize its resources, give its government adequate authority, and overhaul the military establishment and command structure.[25]

On the basis of these instructions, Ambassador Nolting and Diem negotiated a bilateral agreement, and in December both governments announced its nonmilitary features. In a White Paper, basically an appeal for world support, the Department of State declared that North Vietnam had violated the Geneva agreement and that South Vietnam needed assistance. Other nations were asked to help.[26]

Despite these measures, Gen. Curtis E. LeMay, USAF Chief of Staff, believed that the program for South Vietnam was still inadequate. On 5 December 1961 he obtained JCS support for another statement on the need for additional measures. The JCS asked McNamara on 13 January 1962 to inform President Kennedy and Secretary of State Dean Rusk of its belief that the United States should further bolster Diem and discourage factions seeking his overthrow. But Diem would need to cooperate by ending procrastination, authorizing his military commanders to carry out their plans, and providing an adequate basis for U.S. advice and assistance. If, on this basis, the Vietnamese could not control the Viet Cong, U.S. or allied forces should be introduced. In this eventuality, the JCS observed that the war would be peninsular and allow U.S. forces to utilize their experiences in World War II and Korea, the U.S. commitment would not seriously affect operations planned for Berlin and elsewhere, and the Communists could sustain only limited forces because of logistic problems. McNamara sent these views to the President without endorsement, preferring to await the results of the current program.[27]

II. STEPPING UP MILITARY ASSISTANCE

The Kennedy Administration moved rapidly to help the embattled Diem government. On 27 November 1961 McNamara approved the establishment of a new military headquarters, headed by a four-star commander, to manage this country's limited participation in the war. U.S. military men would advise units of the Vietnamese armed forces while they were engaged in combat. U.S. Army helicopters would be sent, plus USAF C-123 transports, T-28 fighters and a tactical air control system. McNamara also asked the JCS to prepare plans to use Vietnamese aircraft and helicopters in defoliant operations.*[1]

This military aid raised an international legal issue, since the Geneva agreement prohibited the acquisition by South Vietnam of modern arms and restricted the size of foreign military advisory groups in that country. The Administration decided to abide by the agreement, but it believed that North Vietnam's violations gave South Vietnam legitimate grounds for self-defense, including accepting U.S. assistance, until these violations ceased. Therefore, the United States would not concede that this aid was a breach of the Geneva agreement.[2]

Establishment of USMAC/V

McNamara's plan to establish a new military headquarters in Saigon stirred considerable debate. The JCS strongly objected to a new headquarters in this area independent of CINCPAC, claiming that this would

---

*Defoliants were chemicals which stripped the leaves of plants. For a discussion of defoliant planning and operations, see pp 56-61.

be incompatible with Admiral Felt's mission and responsibilities. The Joint Chiefs suggested instead the establishment of a subordinate unified command under Felt called "U.S. Forces, Vietnam" with the individual service component commands also in charge of the service sections of the Military Assistance Advisory Group, Vietnam (MAAG/V). As a precondition to altering the command structure, the JCS urged that the United States clearly define its objectives in South Vietnam and extract from the reluctant Diem government a commitment to a joint military program.[3]

The Department of State advocated arrangements less suggestive of major change. It proposed extending the authority of the Chief of MAAG/V over the additional U.S. forces and economic and intelligence activities. State also objected to a four-star commander, believing this would be "an irrevocable and 100 percent commitment to saving South Vietnam."[4]

The conflicting views were reconciled. In mid-December McNamara and Rusk agreed to establish, in accordance with JCS views, a new subordinate unified command under CINCPAC and call it, as State later suggested, the U.S. Military Assistance Command, Vietnam (USMAC/V). The new command would be analagous to the U.S. commands in Taiwan, Korea, and Japan. Its chief would be a four-star commander, a rank McNamara considered "highly essential" to emphasize the "positive impact of change" in U.S. policy.[5]

After Presidential approval and the selection of Army Lt. Gen. Paul D. Harkins as commander, MAC/V was established in Saigon on 8 February

1962. Responsible for carrying out U.S. military policy, Harkins was also authorized to discuss with the Vietnamese all facets of military operations. He reported to the Secretary of Defense through CINCPAC and the JCS. Coequal with the U.S. Ambassador to South Vietnam, Harkins could consult with him on all policy matters. Harkins also provided broad guidance to MAAG/V, now part of his command, on the military assistance program (MAP) for South Vietnam.[6]

USMAC/V was Army-oriented, and this quickly engendered a heated interservice conflict over the conduct of the war and especially over the use and control of airpower. The Air Force had good reason to be disappointed. In early planning, the services had agreed that the Air Force would hold the posts of chief of staff, J-2, and J-5. Harkins, however, selected a Marine lieutenant-general as his chief of staff. As a substitute, he proposed an Air Force officer for J-3, but under Army pressure he chose an Army officer for this post. On 19 February, despite strong remonstrances by LeMay to McNamara and by the Pacific Air Force (PACAF) commander, Gen. Emmett O'Donnell, Jr., to Admiral Felt, the Secretary of Defense approved Harkins' selections.[7]

McNamara promised LeMay he would reconsider this decision if the circumstances warranted, but this prospect appeared dim. The service representation for Headquarters MAC/V was as follows: Army-Commander (Gen.), J-3 (Brig. Gen.), J-4 (Brig. Gen.), and J-6 (Col.); Navy--J-1 (Capt.); Marines--Chief of Staff (Lt. Gen.); and Air Force--J-2 (Col.) and J-5 (Brig. Gen.). Of the five general officers in key positions, the Air Force had only one. Numerically, it also felt underrepresented.

Of the 105 officer spaces initially authorized, the Army had 54, the Navy and Marines 29, the Air Force only 22. Within Headquarters MAAG/V somewhat similar disparities existed.[8]

Establishment of 2d ADVON

The Air Force also had little voice in determining how its air units would function in South Vietnam. Without consultation, Admiral Felt determined that the Chief, Air Force Section, MAAG/V would be responsible for advising and training the VNAF, and he would report to him (Felt) through the Chief, MAAG/V. The Chief, Air Force Section, MAAG/V would also command a special advanced echelon in South Vietnam to provide the VNAF with combat advisory training. He would also command through this echelon scattered PACAF detachments and elements in Southeast Asia. Wearing this second hat, he would report to Felt through O'Donnell, the PACAF commander. Felt emphasized that the title of the advanced echelon should not imply a new command.[9]

On 15 November 1961, Detachment 7, first unofficially and later officially designated 2d ADVON* was established at Tan Son Nhut Airfield near Saigon as a provisional element of the 13th Air Force. Subsequently, it became the only component command of MAC/V when that organization was established. On 20 November Brig. Gen. Rollen H. Anthis, Vice Commander of the 13th Air Force, was named commander of 2d ADVON, and on 1 December, Chief, Air Force Section, MAAG/V.[10]

---

*The detachment was renamed 2d ADVON on 7 June 1962. In this study, it will be cited as 2d ADVON until its redesignation as 2d Air Division in October 1962.

Deployment of USAF Aircraft

Well before MAC/V was established, U.S. military units were deploying to South Vietnam. On 11 October 1961 President Kennedy had authorized the dispatch of the first important USAF unit--Detachment 2--an element of 4400th Combat Crew Training Squadron (Jungle Jim) stationed at Eglin AFB, Fla. On arrival at Bien Hoa Airfield in November, the detachment, nicknamed Farmgate, consisted of eight T-28's, four SC-47's, four B-26's (redesignated RB-26's since the Geneva agreement prohibited the entry of tactical bombers), and 151 officers and airmen. Operational control was vested in 2d ADVON, training in the Air Force Section, MAAG/V, and as indicated, Gen. Anthis commanded both.[11]

The primary mission of Farmgate was to train the Vietnamese in counterguerrilla air tactics and techniques. There were restrictions on combat training operations. Under the rules of engagement approved by the President on 6 December, such operations were authorized only if the VNAF lacked the necessary training and equipment, combined USAF-VNAF crews were aboard, and the missions were confined to South Vietnam. Because of its special role, Farmgate aircraft bore Vietnamese markings.[12]

Since the Geneva agreement prohibited the entry of jets into South Vietnam, the Felt-Nolting proposal,* which the Taylor Mission had supported, was adopted. On 20 October, the Air Force sent four RF-101's and a photo processing cell (PPC) to Tan Son Nhut, ostensibly to photograph areas in the Mekong delta in conjunction with flood relief. Nicknamed Pipestem, these aircraft in 31 days flew 67 reconnaissance sorties over South Vietnam and Laos to fulfill reconnaissance needs.[13]

---

*See p 11.

On 29 October Felt directed PACAF to place four RF-101's and a PPC in Thailand. The aircraft and 45 men from the 45th Tactical Reconnaissance Squadron, 39th Air Division left Misawa, Japan, for Don Muang, Thailand. The unit (known as Able Mable) became operational on 8 November, overlapping briefly and then replacing the Pipestem flights. By the end of 1961, Able Mable had flown 130 sorties over South Vietnam and Laos. It made photos available to theater and national agencies within 24 hours. In February 1962 the unit had 55 men and a new PPC.[14]

In accordance with McNamara's decision of 27 November to accelerate military aid to South Vietnam, the Air Force in December dispatched 16 C-123 TAC transports and 123 men from Pope AFB, N.C., to Clark AB, the Philippines. Nicknamed Mule Train, the squadron arrived at Tan Son Nhut in January 1962 to become the nucleus of an airlift buildup. It airlifted special forces for counterguerrilla operations, airdropped supplies, and trained the Vietnamese.[15]

To conduct defoliation experiments, a group of six C-123's and 69 men (nicknamed Ranch Hand) from TAC's special aerial spray flight at Langley AFB, Va. and Pope AFB, N.C., arrived at Clark in November 1961, then moved to Tan Son Nhut in January 1962. For psychological warfare activities, three USAF SC-47's, specially equipped for leaflet and loudspeaker flights, came to South Vietnam in December 1961 and were quickly operational.[16]

Deployment of Support Equipment

The United States sent support equipment to South Vietnam even before the visit of the Taylor Mission. Headquarters USAF, through the 13th Air Force, surveyed requirements for the radar surveillance equipment needed under the April 1961 program but could not meet them immediately because all available USAF equipment was in use. On 11 September the JCS directed the Air Force to provide a combat reporting center (CRC), an essential element of radar surveillance. A CRC promptly left Shaw AFB, N.C. for Tan Son Nhut, where it went into round-the-clock operation on 5 October. The CRC came under the control of 2d ADVON after that unit was activated in November.[17]

To carry out Taylor Mission recommendations, McNamara on 27 November ordered a tactical air control system (TACS) deployed to South Vietnam. By joint agreement, the Vietnamese and U.S. commanders retained operational control over their own aircraft with operations coordinated through a joint air operations center (JAOC). Activated at Tan Son Nhut on 2 January 1962, the JAOC was command post for 2d ADVON and VNAF and also liaison center with the Army and Navy. It was manned temporarily by 314 PACAF officers and men until regular-duty personnel arrived in February and March 1962.[18]

Established in accordance with a 13th Air Force operational plan (Barndoor), the TACS was assigned to 2d ADVON on 15 January and soon became operational, though with limited capability. In addition to the JAOC and the CRC, the TACS consisted of five forward air controllers (FAC's) at Tan Son Nhut, two air support operations centers (ASOC's)—one in the north with the Vietnamese Army's I Corps at Da Nang, the other in the central highlands with the II Corps at Pleiku—and one combat reporting post (CRP) at Da Nang. When III and IV Corps were established, two ASOC's were added at Can Tho in the south and in Saigon. The various elements of the TACS were interconnected by high-frequency voice and teletype radio circuits.[19]

The radars that controlled friendly aircraft also handled aircraft control and warning (AC&W). In accordance with the Barndoor plan, one USAF-operated AC&W radar was placed at Tan Son Nhut and another at Da Nang, while one VNAF-operated light radar was placed at Pleiku. These radars, plus one installed later at Ubon, Thailand (Barndoor II), provided radar air surveillance of South Vietnam and the surrounding territory.[20]

In January 1962 McNamara and the JCS also decided to establish a troposcatter communication system (Back Porch) under the operating responsibility of the Army. The Air Force installed the "backbone" equipment (AN/MRC-85) at Saigon, Nha Trang, Pleiku, and Da Nang in South Vietnam and at Ubon, Thailand. This equipment, operated by Army and 150 USAF personnel, provided high-quality communications among U.S. military commanders, subordinate commanders, tactical field units, and, as necessary, U.S. or SEATO forces. The Army installed the mobile equipment (AN/TRC-90) for 10 tributary links interconnecting the backbone equipment and provided a signal battalion to operate it. The AN/MRC-85 equipment, installed by 1 September, provided 72 voice channels. The tributary lines added 24 channels. Several months later, under Back Porch II, the Air Force extended the troposcatter system to provide emergency communications between Saigon and Clark AB.[21]

III. PLANS AND OPERATIONS
(December 1961-June 1962)

Operational Planning

As the flow of men and materiel to South Vietnam increased, McNamara and his planners in December 1961 carefully studied short- and long-range operational plans. An early Outline Campaign Plan, drafted by CINCPAC for the Vietnamese, envisaged powerful strikes and the use of defoliants in Zone D of the III Corps area (a region near Saigon overrun by the Viet Cong). The plan also called for blows at guerrilla bases in I and II Corps and border areas and for mopping up and consolidation in central and northern areas.[1]

Since the Vietnamese could neither begin operations in Zone D immediately nor maintain their hold on areas already cleared, McNamara and military officials decided on a simpler plan to gain some initial successes. Known as Operation Sunrise, this plan called for securing and holding Binh Duong Province, where the government controlled only 10 of 46 villages. Based somewhat on successful British operations in Malaya, Operation Sunrise required three months for preparation, four months for military action, and two to three months for consolidation. It was slated to begin on 23 March 1962, and the Vietnamese would undertake shorter-range operations in the interim.[2]

Early in 1962 the Air Force proposed a quick reaction plan that would strengthen the government by demonstrating its concern for the safety of its people. Strongly supported by Zuckert and LeMay, this plan called for a quick reaction force composed of Vietnamese airborne troops and USAF-VNAF transport and strike aircraft deployed in nine areas of the country. Linked by a simple communication system to isolated villages, the force would respond within 10 to 30 minutes to a Viet Cong attack. LeMay thought that the plan would complement the strategic hamlet program* then evolving, which in his opinion was too defensive.3

In March the JCS approved the plan in principle and sent it to CINCPAC. The Army believed that the plan conflicted with the "clear and hold" concept of Operation Sunrise and asked for a Joint Staff study of a substitute plan. Despite strong USAF pressure, Felt believed that there should be only one master counterinsurgency plan for South Vietnam, and he adopted only certain features of the quick reaction plan.4

USAF Operations and Augmentations

Since USAF military units would be exposed to combat, Zuckert was concerned about the problem of public relations. On 4 December 1961, he asked OSD how to deal with possible Communist charges of bacteriological and chemical warfare. OSD responded that all U.S. activities should be explained as training or support for the Vietnamese even if

---

*The Vietnamese government conceived the strategic hamlet program in 1961 and publicly announced support for it in February 1962, but it did not approve a national construction plan until August. Meanwhile, provincial governments built hamlets with little planning or coordination, and many were inadequately fortified and supported.

incidental combat support operations were conducted, and that there should be no comment on reports to the contrary.[5]

U.S. air units began aiding Vietnamese ground troops against the Viet Cong in late 1961. The principal USAF unit, Farmgate, flew its initial combat training sorties on 19 December. Mule Train (C-123) flights began on 3 January 1962; Ranch Hand C-123's began defoliation operations on 13 January. U.S. Army helicopters inaugurated support flights on 23 December 1961, U.S. Marine helicopters in April 1962.[6]

USAF activities fell into two categories: support and tactical. Support included airlift, liaison, observation, rescue, and evacuation; tactical consisted of combat training in close support and interdiction as well as combat airlift and reconnaissance missions. Close air support, provided primarily for the ARVN and Civil Guard, was directed by forward air controllers. Vietnamese requests for interdiction missions often were denied when jungle foliage made identification of friend and foe too difficult. In night operations, flare drops around a village or outpost under attack also deterred guerrillas who feared air strikes.[7]

USAF participation expanded during the first half of 1962 because Operation Sunrise, which began on 23 March, required all types of air support. Farmgate combat training sorties rose from 101 in January to 187 in June; transport and defoliation sorties from 296 to 1,102. Initial defoliation results were encouraging, but the Air Force suspended this type of operation from May to September for political reasons.*[8]

---

*For the discussion of defoliation, see pp 56-61.

There were occasional setbacks. On 11 February an SC-47 on a leaflet-dropping mission crashed, killing eight Americans (six Air Force and two Army) and one Vietnamese. The presence of so many Americans in the aircraft prompted public and Congressional inquiries. At McNamara's request, LeMay studied the psychological warfare mission and decided that the Vietnamese could perform it. The JCS then directed the transfer of the mission to the VNAF as soon as the Vietnamese were trained sufficiently. On 26 May, a Farmgate aircraft hit Da Ket, south of Da Nang, causing civilian casualties. Although the town was improperly marked on a map, military investigators attributed the accident to navigational error and relieved the crew of operational status. The mission was successful otherwise, since it caused an estimated 400 Viet Cong casualties.[9]

Under USAF tutelage, the VNAF increased its combat sorties in A-1H's and T-28's from 150 in January 1962 to 389 in June. The VNAF flew its first T-28 sorties in March. And, in a 50-plane raid on 27 May against a Viet Cong headquarters in the central highlands, the VNAF destroyed warehouses and huts with 100 tons of fire bombs and explosives.[10]

The possibility that enemy aircraft might contest Farmgate-VNAF air superiority led to a new augmentation of USAF strength. On 19-20 March surveillance radar at Pleiku and Man Iang detected unidentified aircraft. Conventional aircraft could not locate them, and PACAF quickly dispatched three F-102 and one TF-102 jet aircraft from Clark AB to Tan Son Nhut where they were placed on alert. Known as Operation Water Glass (redesignated Candy Machine in October 1963), these jets found no hostile aircraft, either at this time or at any time in 1962 and 1963. From April through July 1962 the F-102's deployed to South Vietnam at 10-day intervals, then alternated with a Navy detachment of three AD-5Q aircraft. In late 1962 the F-102's occasionally engaged in psychological warfare by creating sonic booms which disturbed Viet Cong siestas or nighttime sleep.[11]

In May the JCS authorized Sawbuck II, the deployment of a second C-123 transport squadron of 16 aircraft from Pope AFB, N.C., 12 going to Da Nang and 4 temporarily to Thailand. There were now 37 C-123's and 235 USAF personnel in South Vietnam under Mule Train and Sawbuck II. Concurrently, at the direction of the Chief of Staff, TAC established the Tactical Air Transport Squadron (Provisional 2), 464th Troop Carrier Wing, to bring Mule Train, Sawbuck II, and Ranch Hand C-123's under a single commander.[12]

Also in May, an upsurge of Communist attacks in Laos led to the dispatch of four additional night-photo RB-26's, two for Farmgate and two to Thailand. The latter joined Farmgate in December.[13]

The Interdiction Issue

The start of U.S. combat training activities almost immediately created political and military problems. Despite precautions, on 21 February 1962, a Farmgate aircraft erroneously bombed a Cambodian village in a poorly defined border area while participating in a four-day air and ground assault against the Viet Cong. Not only were President Kennedy, the Department of State, and OSD concerned with the ensuing diplomatic difficulties with Cambodia, but they feared that air strikes, if indiscriminate, would antagonize friendly Vietnamese.[14]

The Department of State questioned the wisdom of attacks on villages at all and doubted whether targets were being properly identified. It also alleged that the initial strikes alerted the insurgents, permitting them to escape. State recommended following the methods used successfully by the British in Malaya. The Air Force thought that the air attacks had not been failures because they had attained their objective of clearing the area of guerrillas. Moreover, since the insurgents had a sanctuary nearby, either in North Vietnam, Cambodia, or Laos, the British techniques were not necessarily valid in this instance. O'Donnell expressed his concern to LeMay that this initial reaction against the use of airpower might lead to additional restrictions on Farmgate training missions.[15]

General Anthis, Commander of 2d ADVON, conceded that complete target verification was not always possible since most tactical intelligence and requests for air strikes came from the Vietnamese. However, he defended Farmgate procedures as basically sound. In daytime no targets within five miles of the Laos-Cambodian borders could be attacked, and for night flights, only targets at least 10 miles from the borders. All targets were first marked by a forward air controller. Although McNamara warned against the consequences of harming innocents to kill a few guerrillas and suggested as a rule of thumb that pilots should weigh "risk against gain," he imposed no new rules of engagement on the Farmgate unit.[16]

In March a U.S. Army team that had visited South Vietnam also concluded that indiscriminate bombing played into Viet Cong hands. Because the team failed to substantiate its allegations, no additional curbs were imposed on combat training. The team's additional observations that there were certain target identification problems and that the VNAF flew only daylight sorties were acknowledged by the Air Force which was trying to correct these deficiencies. The Air Force noted, however, that target identification was a problem that applied equally to ground attacks.[17]

PACAF thought that some of the Army charges were motivated by an Army plan to experiment with armed helicopters instead of relying on the VNAF and, when necessary, Farmgate aircraft for top cover and close support. In April LeMay visited South Vietnam and found no basis for "loose statements" which suggested a careless attitude or incorrect procedures. He observed that while the Vietnamese selected the targets, the joint air operations center and air support operations centers carefully checked them, and forward air controllers in liaison aircraft marked them for attack.[18]

IV. PLANS AND OPERATIONS
(July 1962-December 1963)

In mid-1962 the conflict in South Vietnam appeared to many U.S. officials to have reached a turning point. In May McNamara had visited South Vietnam and was "tremendously encouraged," for he found "nothing but progress and hope for the future" in the strategic hamlet and military training programs. Many U.S. military officers were also cautiously optimistic. Although the weekly average of terrorists incidents had declined only slightly--from 414 between October and December 1961 to 394 between April and June 1962--Viet Cong casualties exceeded government casualties by a 5 to 3 ratio. And more guerrillas had surrendered or defected, while government troops had lost fewer weapons.[1]

Planning For An Early Victory

In July 1962 McNamara declared that the period of "crash" military assistance for South Vietnam was ending and that longer-range systematic planning was necessary. Assuming that the insurgency could be checked by the end of 1965, he directed the services to prepare a comprehensive three-year plan for training and equipping the Vietnamese and for removing most U.S. units from South Vietnam. As the Vietnamese assumed responsibility for their own defense, McNamara envisaged removing MAC/V entirely and leaving only a MAAG/V with about 1,600 personnel.[2]

In July McNamara also agreed to the transfer of responsibility for training the Vietnamese civilian irregular defense force (CIDG) from the Central Intelligence Agency to the Department of Defense--specifically to MAC/V. The CIDG was concerned with youth programs, commando units, civic action, and Viet Cong infiltration across the Laotian border.[3]

The services quickly prepared a plan to make the Vietnamese forces largely self-sufficient within three years, and McNamara approved it on 23 August. The plan later was revised extensively and integrated with a five-year U.S. military assistance program (MAP) for the Vietnamese and a national campaign plan (NCP). The Air Force portion of the plan called for accelerated training and equipping of the VNAF.[4]

MAC/V conceived the NCP in October 1962 to encourage the Diem regime to reorganize its military forces and to shorten the war by using its increased military resources in coordinated strikes against the Viet Cong. After the United States persuaded Diem to accept the plan, his government worked out the details aided by U.S. advisors. The NCP also was known as the "explosion" plan since military and paramilitary forces would "explode" into action on many fronts.[5]

The Department of State and the JCS became concerned that the NCP might prove overambitious and fail, undermining Vietnamese morale. MAC/V then scaled it down from a major "detonation" to a series of intense but highly coordinated small operations that would extend the current effort. PACAF believed that the NCP could not fail completely because intensified action against the Viet Cong was bound to assure some success and any offensive would improve military morale and the will to fight.[6]

In accordance with NCP strategy, the Vietnamese would seek out and destroy enemy concentrations, clear and hold liberated areas, and establish fortified strategic hamlets in these areas. Working with plateau and mountain tribesmen, the government forces would achieve better border control. Aircraft would strafe Viet Cong zones, provide close fire support and reconnaissance, and transport men and equipment. The three phases of the NCP included preparation, execution, and consolidation.[7]

During the preparatory phase, Diem on 26 November realigned the military command structure and divided the country into four tactical zones and one military district. The second phase, requiring greatly stepped-up military and paramilitary operations with U.S. support, was scheduled to begin by 28 January 1963, the Vietnamese New Year's Day. But Diem procrastinated and decided not to launch the offensive until two-thirds of the population were in strategic hamlets, weakening the plan.[8]

On 18 June the Vietnamese forces finally received the order to launch the second phase on 1 July. The tempo of military activity then increased somewhat, but there were no spectacular victories. Harkins believed that the NCP had lost much of its usefulness. At the end of August, he informed Diem that government forces had failed to take full advantage of aerial reconnaissance, to pursue the Viet Cong, and to remain in conquered territory. They had fought too many one-day operations and not enough at night, and they had placed too little emphasis on psychological warfare, civic action, and the coordination of intelligence with operations. Responsibility for border surveillance had not been shifted from the special forces to the corps commander, as proposed. And some Vietnamese Army commanders were reluctant to give their troops formal training.[9]

USAF Augmentation

Meanwhile, stepped-up military action and long-range planning required more USAF aircraft and personnel. In August 1962, with JCS approval, four USAF U-10B (L-28) aircraft arrived in South Vietnam to improve air-to-ground communications and target spotting and to provide faster air support. In October Harkins and O'Donnell proposed to augment Farmgate by five T-28's, ten B-26's, two C-47's, and 117 men. McNamara was cool to the proposal because it was contrary to his policy of shifting responsibility to the Vietnamese. But after the JCS affirmed the Harkins-O'Donnell request, he approved it on 28 December and the President concurred shortly afterwards. This boosted Farmgate strength by February 1963 to 41 aircraft and 275 men.[10]

To help carry out the NCP, a second augmentation was approved in March 1963. The Farmgate sortie rate would be increased by 30 to 35 percent. This would be achieved, Felt decided, not by adding new T-28 and B-26 units but by doubling Farmgate personnel. The Army would deploy its own aircraft to support the Vietnamese civilian irregular defense force rather than to rely on additional USAF aircraft, and this triggered a vigorous interservice debate. As a compromise, McNamara and the JCS authorized the Air Force to deploy an additional C-123 squadron (Sawbuck VII), one TO-1D squadron, and place one C-123 squadron on alert. The

Sawbuck VII squadron arrived in South Vietnam in April; the TO-1D squadron, consisting of 22 planes loaned from the Army, in August.[11]

Additional reconnaissance aircraft also were needed. In January 1963 two RF-101's (Patricia Lynn) joined Able Mable (the four RF-101's that had come in November 1961). In March two RB-26C's and two RB-26L's (Sweet Sue) arrived, all capable of taking night photographs. The RB-26L's also had an infrared capability. They were joined in June by two RB-57E's, both outfitted with night photo and infrared equipment. By mid-1963, 12 USAF aircraft and six U.S. Army Mohawks comprised the land-based reconnaissance strength in South Vietnam.[12]

The augmentations and expanded air activity led to personnel and organizational changes. At LeMay's request, the JCS on 12 April reassigned to PACAF for permanent duty the personnel in TAC units (Farmgate, C-123 units, and the new TO-1D squadron) who were on six-month temporary duty. This was done to stabilize manning, reduce training requirements, and make better use of experienced people.[13]

On 17 June Headquarters USAF disestablished Farmgate as a detachment of the Special Air Warfare Center and activated in its place the 1st Air Commando Squadron (Composite) at Bien Hoa Airfield, with Detachment 1 at Plei Ky airport and Detachment 2 at Soc Trang airport. On 8 July the squadron, with an approved strength of 41 aircraft and 474 men, was assigned to 34th Tactical Group, 2d Air Division. On 17 June Headquarters USAF also redesignated the 19th Liaison Squadron, equipped with TO-1D aircraft, as the 19th Tactical Air Support Squadron (Light) and established it at Bien Hoa on 8 July. And on 4 November all USAF reconnaissance aircraft were brought together when PACAF established the 13th Reconnaissance Technical Squadron at Tan Son Nhut.[14]

USAF/VNAF Operations

Farmgate and VNAF units improved old tactics and devised new ones to cope with the Viet Cong. In August 1962 Farmgate crews began furnishing air support through a village air request net. They also discovered that napalm attacks were effective against guerrillas submerged in water, since burning napalm consumed air and forced the insurgents to surface. Farmgate crews also devised a better escort technique for helicopters ferrying Vietnamese troops. Two T-28's flew at different altitudes, permitting better observation and quick-firing passes against the enemy. By dropping colored smoke grenades to mark targets, pilots foiled Viet Cong attempts to confuse them with ordinary smoke grenades.[15]

Guerrilla ambushes of Vietnamese Army vehicle and train convoys had averaged two to three per week during the first half of 1962, but the VNAF significantly reduced this number. At Harkins' suggestion, Diem in August directed his Army commanders to use the VNAF to protect important convoys. Results were immediately gratifying. Between August and October 1962, the commanders made 506 requests for air convoys compared with only 32 for the first seven months of the year. An L-19--or several fighters in very dangerous territory--provided escort and alerted ground troops accompanying the convoys. LeMay called this tactic a "big step forward," and Zuckert noted its success when he testified in February 1963 before a House committee.[16]

With USAF training and assistance, the VNAF improved its employment of aerial flares in night operations. Since these flares deterred the insurgents or forced them to break off attacks against villages and outposts, the VNAF began in August to place C-47 flare aircraft on airborne alert each night.[17]

To improve navigation of USAF and VNAF aircraft, in August the JCS approved installation by the Air Force of a Decca tactical air positioning system, and this British-made low-frequency system went into operation on 15 December. The Decca system, with three ground stations and 50 airborne receivers, provided over-the-horizon coverage and was more accurate than other available systems. A fourth ground station was added in 1963.[18]

The number of USAF sorties increased steadily during the year. Farmgate T-28's and B-26's--averaging a total of only 15 aircraft for the 12-month period--had flown 2,993 operational sorties, C-47's 843 (649 in support of the special forces), and C-123's 11,689. In addition, the transports carried more than 17,000 tons of cargo and air-landed or airdropped 45,000 Vietnamese. Exclusive of jet-aircraft missions, Farmgate, USAF transport, and other operational-type sorties at year's end totaled 15,867.[19]

USAF support constituted, of course, only a portion of all air-power employed. VNAF aircraft and helicopter strength totaled 180 by the close of December 1962, and its A-1H's and T-28's had flown 4,496 sorties during the year. A Marine company with 20 rotary aircraft contributed to the air effort. Of major significance and considerable USAF concern was the expansion of U.S. Army aviation support in South Vietnam.*[20]

---

*For a discussion of Army aviation, see pp 43-46.

Estimates of the damage inflicted by airpower varied. Headquarters USAF concluded that combined Farmgate-VNAF air strikes in 1962 accounted for 28 percent of the 25,100 Viet Cong casualties.* Of this total, Farmgate's T-28's and B-26's inflicted 3,200 and, in addition, destroyed about 4,000 structures and 275 boats. PACAF credited Farmgate aircraft with more than a third of officially recorded guerrilla casualties. The Defense Intelligence Agency attributed 56 percent to all U.S. aircraft employed.[21]

Although these statistics could not be verified easily, the Air Force believed that, by comparing the achievements of the 10,000 members of combined USAF/VNAF units with those of the 400,000 U.S. and Vietnamese Army, Navy, and paramilitary forces, air strikes accounted for a very high rate of enemy casualties in relation to the total effort. After visiting South Vietnam in December, Zuckert concluded that "the type of doctrine that is involved in our air commando operations is proving effective."[22]

In 1963 Farmgate crews trained the VNAF in night and instrument flying to develop an air close support capability during periods of darkness and inclement weather. The VNAF also assumed responsibility for most of the night flare drop missions. On reconnaissance missions, USAF aircraft also located sites for new strategic hamlets and roads. By May, six RF-101's and four RB-26's provided about 70 percent of all targeting information in South Vietnam.[23]

---

*MAC/V estimated the casualties at 30,673 and later at 33,000.

Airborne loudspeakers plus a "Chieu Hoi" or amnesty program, officially proclaimed by the Diem government on 19 April, reportedly encouraged Viet Cong defections. Since the VNAF was not carrying out this form of psychological warfare adequately, McNamara in May authorized USAF crews to participate more directly. At U.S. Army request, Farmgate loudspeaker sorties previously had been reported as "equipment test" missions.[24]

At mid-1963 there were nine loudspeaker aircraft--four USAF, four U.S. Army, and one VNAF. These planes broadcast information on resettlement, amnesty, and strategic hamlets; warned civilians to leave dangerous areas; and carried the voices of defectors. Although results were difficult to measure, most U.S. officials considered the broadcasts useful and desired to increase them.[25]

In September 1963 the Viet Cong began taking advantage of political disorder in Saigon and stepped up the war. After the overthrow of the Diem regime on 1 November,* the insurgents overran scores of inadequately defended strategic hamlets, and government casualties and arms losses mounted. During the week of the coup, the Air Force and the VNAF flew 380 combat and advisory sorties to aid 40 strategic hamlets.[26]

This high sortie rate was maintained through the end of the year. USAF nonjet operational sorties for 1963 totaled more than 42,000, a considerable jump from the nearly 16,000 in 1962. Of the 1963 total, B-26's and T-28's--now averaging an inventory of 25 compared with 15 in 1962--flew 8,522 sorties. Each USAF pilot flew 100 to 150 training sorties

---

*For a discussion of the overthrow, see Ch VIII.

during his 12-month tour of duty. MAC/V estimated that USAF aircraft inflicted about 3,800 of the 28,000 insurgent casualties and destroyed about 5,700 structures and 2,600 boats. VNAF A-1H and T-28 sorties rose to 10,600 in 1963 from about 4,500 in 1962. U.S. Army aviation was employed at an even faster pace with 231,900 sorties claimed in 1963 as compared with 50,000 in 1962.[27]

Low-level air attacks became more hazardous as the accuracy of Viet Cong small arms fire improved. The insurgents scored 89 hits against Farmgate and other USAF planes during the last four months of 1962 but 257 in the first four months of 1963, a three-fold increase. About two-thirds of these were made when the aircraft was below an altitude of 1,000 feet, and some aircraft were lost. On 24 November 1963 the enemy hit 24 U.S. and VNAF aircraft and helicopters, destroying five—a one-day high in the war. During the last three months of the year, 124 USAF and VNAF aircraft were hit, some with .50 caliber weapons. From November 1961 to March 1964, 114 U.S. aircraft were lost in South Vietnam: 34 USAF, 70 Army (including 54 helicopters), and 10 Marine (all helicopters).[28]

As antiaircraft fire, mechanical failure, and difficult terrain increased the aircraft attrition rate in 1963 and contributed to several B-26 and T-28 crashes, some Air Staff officers thought that the rules of engagement for U.S. aircraft should be changed to allow deployment of B-57 and F-100 jets. However, McNamara in March 1964 instead approved an Air Force proposal of September 1963 to replace the B-26's and T-28's with A-1E's.[29]

V. THE DISPUTE OVER AIRPOWER

As air support assumed a greater role in South Vietnam, Air Force-Army tension mounted over its use and control. Disagreements boiled to a head after a Vietnamese attack at Ap Bac, about 30 miles south of Saigon, on 2 January 1963. During the battle, Viet Cong ground fire hit 11 of 15 U.S. Army helicopters supporting the attack, downing five. The enemy inflicted severe losses, killing 65 Vietnamese and three Americans and wounding more than 100 Vietnamese and 10 Americans. For more than an hour, enemy fire pinned down 11 U.S. personnel.[1]

In reviewing the incident, Army officers accused the Vietnamese of lacking aggressiveness and refusing to heed advice. But the Air Force charged that the Army had failed to call on fixed-wing aircraft for cover becaust it was carrying out a close-support test of its armed helicopters. The two services could not agree on the reasons for the defeat.[2]

The JCS Review

Because of this disagreement, McNamara and the JCS decided on 7 January to send to South Vietnam a team of senior JCS and service representatives headed by the Army Chief of Staff, Gen. Earle G. Wheeler. Before the team left, service briefings laid bare doctrinal differences over the use of airpower in counterinsurgency operations. The Air Force believed that its system could meet any counterinsurgency requirements for reconnaissance, quick reaction, close support, air cover for helicopters or convoys, delivery of airborne troops and supplies, casualty evacuation, and communications. The Army, conversely, maintained that it alone should be responsible for counterinsurgency since its organic air arm, weapons, and tactics were especially suited for land operations. It viewed the work of USAF's Special Air Warfare Center as trespassing on a mission traditionally assigned to the Army and Marines. The lessons learned about airpower in World War II and Korea, it argued, did not necessarily apply to South Vietnam where aircraft did not need to be as fast and where they needed to be based near the target. The Army demanded decentralized control of airpower in order to use its own support aircraft, whereas the Air Force wanted centralized control. Army and Air Force definitions of "close support" clearly differed.[3]

The JCS team went to South Vietnam, assessed military operations, and concluded in February that the United States should maintain its current level of aid for the Diem government and follow the three-year comprehensive plan for phasing out U.S. support. In commenting on the use of airpower, the team said that the Harkins-Anthis relationship was satisfactory but there were weaknesses in joint planning of air activities, reporting helicopter movements, and conducting logistic airlift. The team offered to furnish Harkins with experts to resolve airlift problems, but it thought that the joint planning and reporting difficulties could be ironed out at lower levels.[4]

In a separate report, the USAF team representative, Lt. Gen. David A. Burchinal, Deputy Chief of Staff for Plans and Programs, Headquarters

USAF, noted that the solution in South Vietnam depended on military, political, and economic factors, and he was less optimistic about an early victory. The Administration should cancel political restrictions and operations outside South Vietnam and on crop destruction. It should also give more authority to the American Ambassador in Saigon and to MAC/V. In the air war, Burchinal foresaw the need for jet aircraft, since conventional aircraft would become more vulnerable to Viet Cong automatic weapons. He recommended to Wheeler the return of test projects to the United States, removal of Howze Board issues,* and a curb on the Army's generation of air requirements. Burchinal believed that all aviation units should report to the JAOC, that armed helicopters should not be deployed until their usefulness had been determined, and that they then should operate under the same rules of engagement as Farmgate aircraft. He also urged assignment of a three-star USAF air deputy to the MAC/V staff, and the establishment of Army and Navy component commands similar to the 2d Air Division.[5]

As a result of the JCS team review, the Air Force won minor concessions, such as four more officer spaces on the MAC/V staff and Army support for an air deputy commander. But the limits and restraints on Farmgate operations remained in effect because the Administration was

---

*The Army Tactical Mobility Board (known as the Howze Board after its chief, Lt. Gen. Hamilton H. Howze) recommended on 31 July 1962 that the U.S. Army assume part of the tactical close support mission. The board proposed that the Army obtain large numbers of fixed-wing aircraft, including transports and helicopters, and be responsible for their use and control. To the Air Force, this meant an encroachment upon a traditional USAF mission.

determined not to risk escalating the war and the Army largely controlled the U.S. military effort in South Vietnam.[6]

The Interdiction Issue Again

In March 1963 the Department of State again raised the subject of interdiction. Observing that Farmgate training aircraft flew numerous sorties of this type each month, W. Averill Harriman, Assistant Secretary of State for Far Eastern Affairs, solicited the views of Ambassador Nolting in Saigon. Harriman thought that air interdiction should be employed only against clearly defined enemy territory. He conceded that targeting procedures had improved and that no reliable information had indicated any undesirable effects. But he stressed the political nature of the war, Vietnamese resentment against air strikes that might aid Viet Cong recruitment, the unsuccessful interdiction experience of the French, the political unawareness of provincial and district chiefs who supplied target information, and the restrictions of the 1954 Geneva agreement. To Harriman, the basic question was the political cost versus the military advantage of interdiction, whether by U.S. or Vietnamese pilots.[7]

Headquarters USAF considered the Harriman analysis as not wholly accurate and representing the views of only a small but influential minority in the State Department. The Air Staff especially disagreed that the war was only political or that occasional harm to innocents created a military problem. USAF planners thought that the State Department officials should study ground combat as well as air action when they assessed the effects of civilian casualties. The airmen noted that the small Farmgate-VNAF force had caused an important percentage of Viet Cong casualties. In April, Ambassador Nolting's reply to Harriman dispelled USAF concern. He recommended continuation, where necessary, of Farmgate interdiction-type sorties to restrict enemy movements, supplement VNAF efforts, and aid the national campaign plan.[8]

Because the interdiction issue again had been raised, Gen. Anthis in May explained again to U.S. officials the detailed and time-consuming method used to select and confirm targets. In interdiction sorties flown since January 1962, the targets selected were primarily enemy concentrations or buildings either used by the Viet Cong or abandoned by Vietnamese who had moved to strategic hamlets. By day, Farmgate crews hit targets only when marked by a VNAF forward air controller; by night, only targets illuminated by a C-47 flare ship in radio contact with Vietnamese ground forces. Military officials investigated all reports of targeting errors and, of 10 recent allegations, had verified only two.[9]

Although a State Department representative expressed concern about Farmgate combat training, McNamara made no comment. In May 1963 OSD and the JCS decided not to take any further action on this issue for the time being, but the Air Force expected that it would come up again.[10]

The Problem of Army Aviation

Despite the steadily-rising Farmgate sortie rate, the Air Force believed that the full potential of its air resources was not being employed. One reason was the rules of engagement that clearly limited USAF participation. Combat training sorties were permitted only if the

VNAF lacked the necessary training and equipment and if combined USAF-VNAF crews were on board. There were also the time-consuming target identification procedures. In July 1962 PACAF urged that the provision requiring the presence of a Vietnamese crew member be rescinded, but Headquarters USAF could not overcome State and OSD objections.[11]

The major obstacle to the enlargement of the Air Force role in South Vietnam, however, was the U.S. Army. Its aviation arm, consisting of Mohawk, Caribou, and liaison aircraft and helicopters, grew by December 1962 to about 200 while the Air Force had only 63. In its support role, the Army frequently followed Howze Board concepts and used its aircraft outside the centralized tactical air control system (TACS) rather than call upon Farmgate and VNAF units. This practice brought the Army into a continuing, abrasive conflict with the Air Force.[12]

After examining the TACS in operation, Lt. Gen. Gabriel P. Disosway, Deputy Chief of Staff for Operations, Headquarters USAF, concluded in December that its potential was high. He decried the Army practice of ignoring it because this led, in effect, to two separate tactical air control systems--one Air Force, the other Army. The Air Force thought that centralized control was a necessity. In a special forces attack on 10 August, for example, the Army had neither planned nor called upon the TACS for air cover, and the Viet Cong had escaped.[13]

Another problem arose when USAF air liaison officers (ALO's) were assigned to ARVN divisions to advise them on air support. The Army insisted that these ALO's advise only the U.S. Army senior advisor to the ARVN commander. This dispute was fundamental, since it could determine whether Farmgate and VNAF or U.S. Army aviation would be employed for specific operations. Starting in mid-1962 USAF and Army leaders in South Vietnam tried to resolve this issue, but they had not succeeded by the end of 1963.[14]

In November 1962 Headquarters USAF acknowledged the lack of timely and accurate air intelligence and quick, reliable response to requests for air support. It ascribed this partly to inadequate delegation of authority within the Vietnamese forces, slow development of the VNAF, and insufficient Vietnamese appreciation of and confidence in tactical airpower. But the Air Staff added that two contributing factors were the assignment of only Army intelligence advisors—28 in all—to the single intelligence agency responsible for targeting and the requirement that forward air controllers report through an airborne air controller rather than directly to strike aircraft.[15]

The Air Force also believed that the Army did not comply fully with the rules of engagement. Farmgate pilots, complying with combat training rules, flew in VNAF-marked aircraft, always carried a Vietnamese crew member, and received no official publicity. Army Mohawk and armed helicopter pilots seemed to interpret the rules more freely and engaged in close support missions, flew in U.S.-marked aircraft, often did not carry a Vietnamese crew member, and received official publicity.[16]

When U.S. forces began to support air-ground operations, USAF and VNAF ground communications for tactical air control were grossly incompatible with those of the Army. As a consequence, the services decided early in 1962 to retrofit AN/ARC-44 sets on all aircraft. But the Army, which administered the procurement contract, gave first priority to retrofitting its own aircraft rather than those of the Air Force and VNAF. After the OSD and JCS interceded, the Army agreed in June 1963 to meet the needs of the U.S. and Vietnamese Air Forces.[17]

The two services also differed as to whether the Army's Caribou was preferable to the larger C-123 in counterinsurgency operations. The Army using its own parameters "proved" that the Caribou was more suitable because it could use 147 airfields in South Vietnam and the C-123 only 70. USAF analyses disproved this assertion.[18]

Despite USAF objections, the role of Army aviation in South Vietnam continued to expand. On 8 July 1963, MAC/V tightened Army control of air operations by establishing an aviation headquarters in each Vietnamese corps to plan and control Army and Marine aviation supporting it. In December the Army had 325 airplanes, or 47 percent of the 681 employed in South Vietnam. The Air Force had 117, the VNAF 228, and the Marines 20.[19]

Problems of Command Relations

The Air Force strongly believed that it could remove some of the restraints on USAF activities if it obtained a larger voice in the councils of the Army-dominated MAC/V. In April 1962, during a JCS meeting with McNamara, LeMay had charged that air planning often was omitted, that Anthis had difficulty seeing Harkins, and that neither Harkins nor his Chief of Staff, Marine Corps Maj. Gen. Richard G. Weede, properly understood air operations.[20]

Felt replied that Harkins and Weede were superior officers who were fully experienced in air-ground tactics and that Anthis could see Harkins

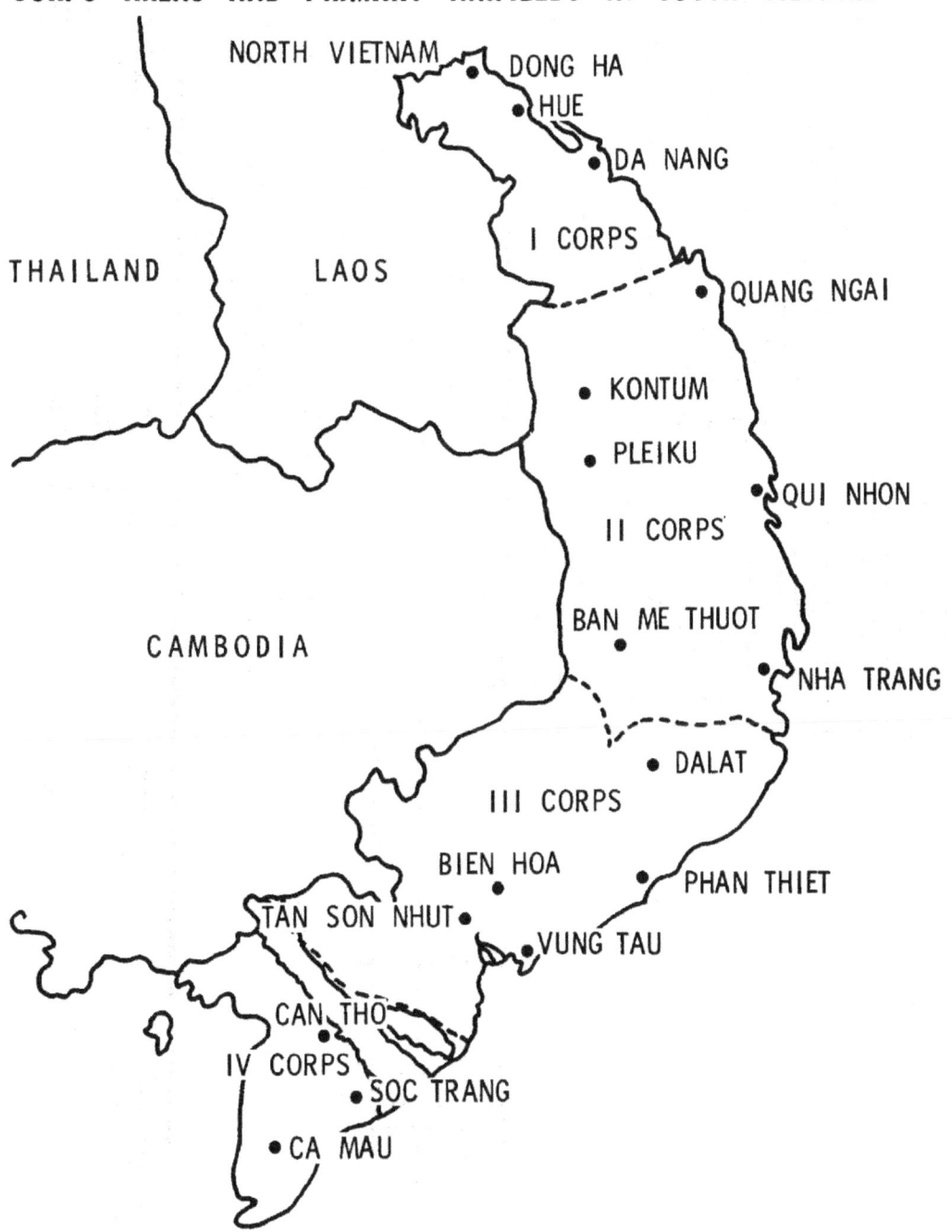

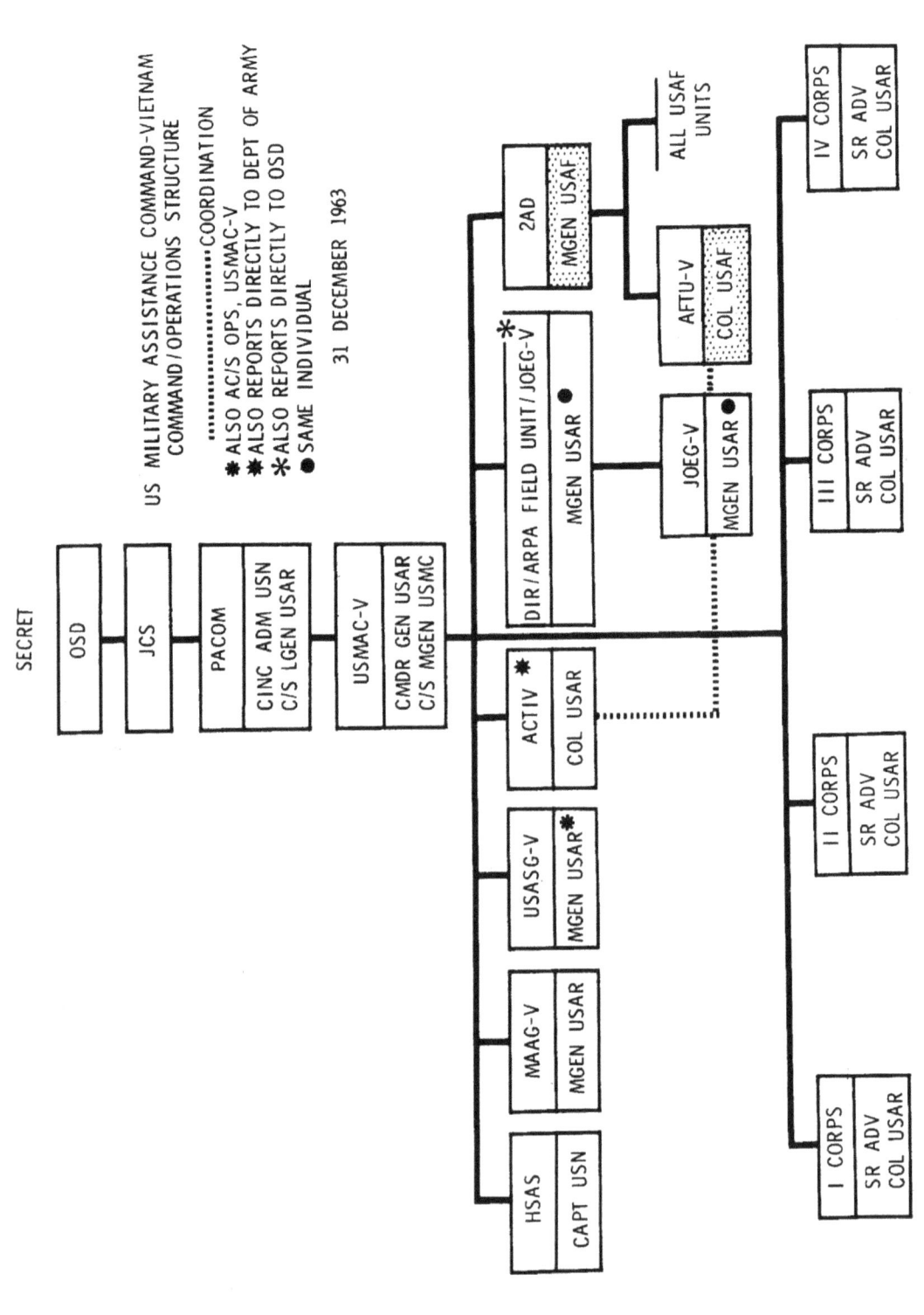

at any time. He acknowledged inadequacies but noted that the VNAF was learning quickly and that the occasions when airpower was not used but should have been were exceptions rather than the rule.[21]

Felt's detailed control also chafed the Air Force, since he assigned air units to MAC/V and fragmented USAF units among subordinate elements, limiting the responsibilities of both O'Donnell and Anthis. O'Donnell's primary authority consisted largely of providing logistic support or correcting problems reported by 13th Air Force or 2d ADVON. Gen. Disosway observed in December 1962 that the Air Staff did not always understand this.[22]

Since the Air Force had been denied the posts of chief of staff and chief of J-3, it urged the assignment of a three-star Air Force deputy commander to Harkins. Harkins and Felt agreed, and the JCS concurred on 22 August 1962, but McNamara decided in October that such a post was unnecessary. The Air Force then tried to secure the post of chief of staff when the Marine incumbent departed. But the Marine Corps adamantly opposed this, and the effort was abandoned. As noted earlier,* the JCS team review early in 1963 resulted in four more officer spaces for the Air Force, two in J-3 and two in J-4, but this was considerably less than it desired.[23]

In September Harkins and Felt agreed that the post of chief of staff should be filled by an Air Force general on 1 June 1964. They also agreed that five more administrative slots should go to USAF personnel. The JCS approved their decisions on 7 November. On 2 December, however, President Johnson directed the JCS to certify only "blue ribbon" men

---

*See p 41.

to MAC/V. After this injunction and another visit to South Vietnam, McNamara approved on 6 January 1964 the designation of Army Lt. Gen. William C. Westmoreland as deputy commander and the transfers of J-1 from the Navy to the Army and J-2 from the Air Force to the Marine Corps. In the latter instance, the Air Force chief of J-2 was downgraded to deputy J-2 and, on orders of LeMay, reassigned.[24]

At the end of 1963 the Army held six of the nine top positions on the MAC/V staff (commander, deputy commander, J-1, J-3, J-4, and J-6), the Marine Corps two (chief of staff and J-2), and the Air Force one (J-5). Of 335 positions allocated in early 1964, the Army held 199, the Air Force 75, the Navy 42, and the Marine Corps 19. The Army was now in firmer control of planning and operations in South Vietnam than before. Reflecting this preeminent position, the Army had about 10,100 of the nearly 16,000 U.S. troops in the country at the end of 1963. The Air Force had 4,600, the Navy and Marine Corps 1,200.[25]

VI. TESTING CONCEPTS AND WEAPONS

As part of the program of action approved on 29 April 1961, President Kennedy authorized a combat development test center (CDTC) in South Vietnam. Composed of Americans and Vietnamese, CDTC was placed under the Vietnamese Joint General Staff in Saigon. In August it began experimenting with various projects, including the use of chemicals to destroy jungle foliage. The Americans in its field unit were members of OSD's Advanced Research Projects Agency (ARPA).[1]

On 5 September McNamara informed the services and other U.S. agencies that he wished South Vietnam to be a "laboratory for the development of organization and procedures for the conduct of sublimited war." Some "laboratory" activities quickly became Army-Air Force combat test programs that engendered heated controversy over the use of tactical airpower.[2]

Supervision of Testing

To the Air Force, the Army desire to "verify" its Howze Board concepts by testing its aircraft in combat support in South Vietnam was an attempt to preempt certain traditional USAF roles and missions. In July 1962 LeMay proposed that a joint operational evaluation group (JOEG/V) in South Vietnam conduct meaningful tests to meet stated objectives. He hoped thereby to restrain the Army from introducing air units and equipment into Southeast Asia under the guise of testing. The JCS agreed, and on 21 July Felt established the group under the operational control of Harkins. Under its terms of reference, the JOEG/V would approve or disapprove test proposals by the JCS, the services, and other agencies. It would evaluate only combat tests having joint service implications.³

Since the ARPA Field Unit of CDTC was outside U.S. military channels, the JCS proposed that it too be placed under Harkins' operational control. McNamara decided instead to combine the administration of the unit and JOEG/V and create the post of director for both. The JCS and Harold Brown, OSD's Director of Defense Research and Engineering (DDR&E), selected Army Brig. Gen. Robert A York for the post, and McNamara approved his terms of reference on 31 October. York was responsible to Brown for CDTC activities and to Felt, through Harkins, for evaluating military operations and tests. All commands and services coordinated their tests both with York and the Vietnamese, included York's conclusions on test results, and made them available to the proper agencies.⁴

This centralized supervision of testing proved short-lived. On 11 September 1962 Secretary of the Army Cyrus R. Vance proposed establishment of a separate Army test unit in South Vietnam. LeMay opposed this move vigorously in the JCS, arguing that it would duplicate JOEG/V functions, result in narrow conclusions, and permit the Army to transgress upon traditional USAF missions of close support, escort of airborne forces, and combat air cargo. The Navy and Marine Corps sympathized with the Army proposal, however. Felt also concurred with the Army, provided that the test personnel and equipment remain in South Vietnam only for the duration of the project. In October McNamara formally approved the Army plan.⁵

Headquarters USAF then weighed various PACAF suggestions and decided that the Air Force also needed a special unit in South Vietnam to test concepts, tactics, aircraft, ordnance, and support equipment. These would complement but not duplicate special air warfare tests at Eglin AFB, Fla. Acting under OSD and JCS directives, LeMay in January 1963 ordered the establishment of a 12-man test unit as a special staff section within the 2d Air Division.[6]

The Army Concepts Testing in Vietnam (ACTIV) was established in November 1962 as a permanent unit that would require initially 97 men. Since the Air Force would have a test unit also, Felt objected to this size. He approved the deployment of ACTIV on 7 January 1963 only after its roster had been trimmed to 60 and additional personnel assigned on a temporary basis. Sharing somewhat the Air Force view on this matter, Felt informed the JCS that the use of South Vietnam as a "test bed" was beclouding the primary U.S. objective of assisting the war effort.[7]

The JCS team that visited Vietnam early in 1963 decided that there were too many test organizations and projects in that country and that their contributions should be appraised by MAC/V.[8] In his separate report, Burchinal recommended, as had others in the Air Staff, that all testing be withdrawn from Vietnam since it disrupted the task of defeating the Viet Cong. Subsequently, LeMay urged vigorously but unsuccessfully that U.S. Strike Command test divergent service concepts and doctrines. He decried interservice debates in the presence of an ally. He also pointed out that the Army did not withdraw its test units, thus adding to costs and logistic problems.[9]

Felt agreed with the JCS team that he and Harkins were in the best position to determine the validity of a test project. If they did not agree, the decision could go to the JCS; if ARPA desired a project despite JCS recommendations, the decision could rest with the Secretary of Defense. With the consent of DDR&E, the JCS submitted a similar recommendation to McNamara who approved it on 23 April.[10]

In May the JCS asked Felt to prepare new terms of reference for consolidating combat development with research and development testing and engineering. The JCS then became deadlocked over an Air Force proposal to rotate the position of chief of this combined activity among the services and an Army proposal to delete a requirement that the JCS settle test problems affecting roles and missions. The Army objected to the first proposal because of its predominance in Vietnam, the Air Force to the second because only in the JCS did it possess a strong voice—and possible veto—on measures vital to its interests. And when Felt recommended that the combined activity be placed within military channels under Harkins, this was opposed by ARPA which favored a joint field agency with the commander responsible to both ARPA and Harkins.[11]

Reluctant to send a split paper to McNamara, the JCS finally asked its Chairman, General Maxwell Taylor, to decide upon the terms of reference. Taylor accepted some Air Force suggestions, but in the key decision he sided with the Army by deleting the requirement that projects with roles and mission implications be submitted to the JCS for approval. This gave CINCPAC rather than the JCS responsibility for settling such matters. In early January 1964 the terms of reference went to OSD.[12]

Test Results

The Army began unilateral testing in late 1962; the Air Force, in early 1963. In conjunction with combat or special forces operations, the Army evaluated the Mohawk, armed helicopters, and the Caribou. In his February report, Burchinal declared that the Mohawk tests were designed to show how this aircraft could perform at less cost the USAF missions of artillery spotting, fire adjustment, reconnaissance, airborne command and control, and flank security. He believed that a test of this plane under combat conditions was unnecessary and added that USAF experience demonstrated that Army field maintenance for the Mohawk was unduly expensive and inefficient.[13]

After the JOEG/V-ARPA Field Unit evaluated the Mohawk tests, the JCS split over the conclusions. The Air Force disagreed that the Mohawk had "fully documented" its offensive capability and that Army direct, decentralized control showed better results than the centralized control exercised by the TACS. The Air Force also objected that the JOEG/V-ARPA Field Unit had violated its terms of reference by commenting on doctrinal issues. Moreover, it stated that the unit's comparisons with other aircraft operating under different rules with different missions were invalid.[14]

Burchinal also had considered Army tests of armed helicopters to be of dubious value because no fixed-wing aircraft were employed for making comparisons. Army statistics on antiaircraft hits had omitted flying time and failed to differentiate between combat and combat-support sorties. LeMay pointed to the vulnerability of helicopters to ground fire, their weakness as "firing platforms," and the Marine Corps desire for fixed-wing aircraft as cover for its helicopters.[15]

The JOEG/V-ARPA Field Unit concluded, however, that armed helicopters were the most effective, single, aerial system for counterinsurgency and that they should provide the additional close support that fixed-wing aircraft could not give. Harkins thought the evidence insufficient to support the first conclusion, and Felt questioned the statistics indicating armed helicopters effectively suppressed ground fire. The Air Force questioned both conclusions. The JCS agreed with the critics but split over whether the tests indicated a requirement for armed helicopters to protect transport helicopters. The Air Force believed, of course, that they did not.[16]

In December, the JOEG/V-ARPA Field Unit concluded that the Army's Caribou tests demonstrated this transport's "extremely advantageous" characteristics for counterinsurgency, citing its short take-off and landing capabilities, light wheel pressure, and load adaptability. According to the testers, the Caribou could use air strips in the Mekong delta that heavier aircraft could not. They claimed that the Caribou was no more comparable to the C-123 than a two and a half-ton truck to a five-ton truck. On the merits of centralized versus decentralized control of the Caribou, they maintained that aircraft near a field commander were more responsible than those removed from his control. By the end of the year the JCS had not completed its study of this evaluation, but it was clear that the Air Force would not agree.[17]

Meanwhile, the Air Force unit had tested the YC-123H,* the U-10, and the Decca tactical air positioning system (TAPS).+ It concluded that the YC-123H could fulfill most airlift requirements in South Vietnam, operate from 88 percent of the airfields in that country, and almost satisfy the long-standing requirement for a 10-ton short take-off and landing aircraft with a 500 nautical-mile radius. The JOEG/V-ARPA Field Unit accepted this assessment but noted that Harkins believed this plane complementary to the Caribou, while the Air Force deemed it competitive.[18]

USAF testers decided that the U-10 was excellent for psychological warfare, support airlift, visual and manually controlled reconnaissance, and short take-off and landing. Forward air controllers had found it unsuitable, however, as it was also vulnerable to ground fire, had poor cockpit arrangements, and was not sufficiently maneuverable at high speeds. The JOEG/V-APRA Field Unit did not disagree.[19]

Tests of the TAPS indicated that it was promising but that its MK VII airborne equipment had experienced a major malfunction. As a consequence, the JOEG/V-ARPA Field Unit stated tentatively that the system was unreliable. Before it reached a definite concludion, it awaited completion of ACTIV tests to determine whether TAPS was adaptable to helicopter operations.[20]

---

*The YC-123H was a modified C-123B capable of short-field take-off and landing.

+For the introduction of this system into South Vietnam, see p 35.

At LeMay's direction, the 13th Air Force used operational records to make tactical analyses of other USAF aircraft. The analysts assessed the T-28B as extremely effective and the B/RB-26 as effective also. But both planes were hindered by stringent target identification requirements, a shortage of VNAF crew members, and incompatible air-ground communication equipment. The analysts described the B/RB-26 as deficient in maneuverability, rate of climb, and dive angle capability, but they recommended its retention until the Air Force could replace it with a more suitable aircraft.[21]

To the analysts, the C-123B was a successful airplane and its replacement by the Caribou would be economically unsound and detrimental to counterinsurgency operations. They found that the TF-102 had demonstrated its identification capability in daylight.[22]

PACAF proposed a test of USAF tactical air support concepts, and the Air Staff in September 1963 requested that command to make the necessary preparations. This test would provide statistics on reaction times, responsiveness, and results of air strikes based on requests that used the USAF-operated TACS.[23]

Despite its interest in these tests, Headquarters USAF remained strongly convinced that testing in South Vietnam should cease because it interfered with the conduct of counterinsurgency operations. But OSD and the other services disagreed.[24]

Defoliation

The United States not only tested the effectiveness of defoliation as a counterinsurgency technique but also conducted defoliant operations against the Viet Cong. The spraying of jungle vegetation and crops had a twofold objective--reducing the danger of enemy ambushes and denying food to the Viet Cong. CDTC began testing in August 1961 but no large-scale operational plans were drawn up until after the Taylor Mission. On 21 November, Deputy Defense Secretary Roswell L. Gilpatric outlined for President Kennedy a carefully-controlled defoliation plan that was designed to support CINCPAC's Outline Campaign Plan.* To guard against ambushes, he proposed spraying a swath 200 yards wide on each side of the principal roads between Saigon and other key cities, roads peripheral to Zone D (the area near Saigon controlled by the Viet Cong), and Cambodian border areas through which guerrillas infiltrated. Gilpatric advocated spraying to deny food only after the friendly population had been resettled and fed. Six USAF C-123's would carry out tactical and border-control operations and specially-equipped Vietnamese helicopters, similar to those used by the British in Malaya in 1953, would destroy crops. He estimated that the program would cost $8 to $10 million dollars.[25]

Administration officials debated how the defoliation missions should be carried out. OSD and JCS favored open participation by aircraft and crews carrying USAF designations. The State Department, apprehensive about possible criticism by the International Control Commission, desired aircraft with Vietnamese markings and USAF crews in civilian attire. It was finally agreed that defoliation missions flown by USAF aircraft and crews should carry a Vietnamese crew member. Vietnamese markings were used only on a few special occasions. In Saigon, MAAG/V

---

*See p 22.

and Vietnamese officials worked out details of the Gilpatric plan. Harkins believed that defoliants would be effective in Zone D which had relatively few people, but Ambassador Nolting thought that their use might alert the Viet Cong. In December they agreed that defoliants could aid but not "win the battle" in that zone, and the Outline Campaign Plan was changed accordingly.[26]

Meanwhile, the Air Force deployed six C-123's and 69 men from TAC's Aerial Spray Flight at Langley AFB, Va., and Pope AFB, N.C. The aircraft, crews, and support personnel reached Clark AB on 6 November, and in January 1962 they proceeded to Tan Son Nhut Airfield. On 13 January three C-123's begain spraying along 16 miles of a road between Bien Hoa and Vung Tau. They did not spray in Zone D since this was declared temporarily impractical.[27]

As expected, Viet Cong propagandists attributed all dying plants to the spraying and warned that the chemicals had harmful effects. Certain Vietnamese claimed property damage from spraying, and a Vietnamese board evaluated the claims. Some were valid, some were not. Ambassador Nolting feared that unsuccessful claimants might become antagonistic.[28]

In May 1962 Harkins reported that in 21 areas sprayed, air-to-ground visibility had improved by 70 percent, ground visibility by 60. He thought that the C-123's could have achieved even better results with improved spraying gear and more herbicides. A subsequent evaluation indicated that defoliants were particularly useful in destroying mangrove but their effects had been overestimated in areas of mixed vegetation. Felt urged the JCS to authorize the spraying of grass, weeds, and brush around depots, airfields, and fields of fire. In the delta, 112 guerrillas had been frightened by defoliants and had surrendered, and Felt asked for an evaluation of psychological effects. He believed that in the future only three C-123's would be needed for defoliant operations.[29]

Communist propaganda and international negotiations on Laos prompted President Kennedy on 2 May to halt defoliation in South Vietnam temporarily and direct that testing continue in Thailand. The C-123's resumed spraying in South Vietnam from 3 September to 11 October and achieved excellent results, according to the JCS, by using more herbicides and larger droplets. In six different areas, these sprayings using three gallons of defoliant per acre killed about 95 percent of the vegetation within 10 days. When one gallon per acre had been used in earlier operations, it took 20 to 60 days to obtain similar results.[30]

Because of these successful tests, the JCS recommended the following: (1) authority for Nolting and Harkins to order non-crop destruction projects; (2) defoliation around four communication routes and one power line; (3) additional testing of improved chemicals, dispersal equipment, and delivery techniques in the United States and the Panama Canal Zone; and (4) more attention to psychological aspects.[31]

On 13 October Gilpatric agreed with the JCS that testing outside South Vietnam was necessary and that psychological aspects deserved more attention. He noted that DDR&E was stepping up research with herbicides. And on 27 November President Kennedy approved the other recommendations by authorizing Nolting and Harkins to order destruction of vegetation, except crops, and by designating five new areas as defoliation targets.[32]

Meanwhile, crop destruction plans had been intensively reviewed. McNamara, Felt, Harkins, and Nolting favored a trial project, the spraying of 2,500 acres in Phu Yen province, but Secretary of State Rusk and Assistant Secretary Harriman were opposed. Rusk thought there was insufficient evidence that the crops belonged to the Viet Cong, feared adverse international reaction, and warned that a premature program could prompt the Viet Cong to step up attacks against strategic hamlets. Observing that the way to win a guerrilla war was to win the support of the people, Rusk argued that crop destruction ran counter to this rule. At best, he thought it should be attempted only in the latter stages of an anti-guerrilla campaign.[33]

By the late summer of 1962 the maturity of crops and continued State Department opposition led to abandonment of the plan for spraying crops in large areas of Phu Yen. Shortly afterwards, however, a limited program was approved for Phu Yen and Thau Thien provinces, which included spraying crops abandoned by Montagnard tribesmen to prevent their use by the Viet Cong. Thereafter, because of the delay in getting JCS approval and the advent of the dry season, there were no spraying projects until February 1963 when they were resumed until May. During this latter period, in accordance with Felt's recommendation, the number of USAF spray-equipped C-123's was cut to three and support personnel to seven officers and 12 enlisted men.[34]

In April the JCS summarized defoliation operations since their inception. The aircraft had sprayed along 87 miles of roads and canals, around military installations, and on 104 acres of crops in two provinces.

Herbicides had destroyed about 756,000 pounds of food without adverse effects on friendly Vietnamese. Conceding that it was difficult to measure military effectiveness precisely, the JCS thought that the benefits to reconnaissance from improved visibility and enhanced security made defoliation desirable and urged its continuation. The JCS believed that proper counter-propaganda actions would offset any adverse Communist charges.[35]

On 7 May, however, new State-OSD guidelines on defoliation contained so many restrictions that few operations were conducted afterwards. The Department of State basically opposed defoliation, especially crop destruction, because it might have adverse effects on friendly Vietnamese which the Communists could exploit. A small project was carried out in June, but a request to spray a 3,000-acre crop area was not approved at year's end. Ambassador Nolting and Felt again vouched for the usefulness of defoliation and recommended it as more efficient than the Vietnamese practice of burning, pulling, or cutting, but noted that the time-consuming procedures required for obtaining approval of defoliation missions negated their effectiveness. Because of the political restrictions and the limited period during the year that defoliation operations could be carried out, at the end of 1963, some military officials were seriously considering abandonment of the whole program.[36]

VII. USAF SUPPORT OF THE VIETNAMESE AIR FORCE

When the United States decided in late 1961 to step up its military assistance to South Vietnam, Headquarters USAF faced the task of enlarging an extremely small Republic of Vietnam Air Force. Some reasons for the VNAF's limited capability were inherent, such as the difficulty of quickly training poorly-educated Vietnamese. But the Air Force believed that another reason for VNAF weakness was the fact that the Army-dominated MAAG/V failed to appreciate the important role airpower could play in counterinsurgency. For example, the January 1961 agreement to increase the Vietnamese armed forces by 20,000 men included only about 500 spaces for the VNAF. Again, the border patrol proposed in the April program of action led to no immediate decision on VNAF employment. In mid-1961 the Air Force thought that VNAF's 4,765 men and 142 aircraft were much too small a part of a total Vietnamese military strength of about 170,000.*[1]

A Vietnamese Army Air Force?

The U.S. Air Force was disturbed by U.S. Army efforts to encourage the Army of Vietnam to establish its own air force. In September 1961 U.S. and Vietnamese diplomatic and military representatives, including President Diem, agreed to form ARVN aviation units. U.S. Army officials then planned to transfer some VNAF aircraft to ARVN to carry out this agreement.[2]

---

*See pp 6-7.

When McNamara asked the JCS in October to review this proposal, that body could not reach an agreement. The proposal contravened long-established Air Force doctrine, and LeMay objected vigorously. He argued that the VNAF's administration, logistic, and maintenance responsibilities could not be separated from its operational activities. If divided, it could delay massing available airpower against a large opposing force. And, if the forces of the Southeast Asia Treaty Organization entered the war, an air component would be needed to control all airpower that might be used.[3]

In December Felt asserted, and O'Donnell agreed, that "team work" rather than reorganization was necessary. McNamara then decided against an ARVN air corps, but he added that the VNAF needed to become more responsive to the requirements of ARVN corps commanders. Nevertheless, MAAG/V and then MAC/V continued to encourage the formation of an ARVN air corps, but without success.[4]

Buildup of the VNAF

The Air Force provided aircraft, helicopters, and training personnel for the VNAF. Since USAF T-28B's were not immediately available, the U.S. Navy, in December 1961, sent the VNAF 16 T-28C's and training personnel. The aircraft remained in the inventory. By April 1962, however, the Air Force had supplied the Vietnamese with 30 T-28B's, a 52-man T-28 training unit, and 30 C-47 aircraft and pilots. Besides training VNAF personnel to fly C-47's, these pilots airlifted livestock to Vietnamese outposts, quickly earning the sobriquet of "dirty thirty." They served until December 1963, logging about 20,000 flying hours.[5]

In April 1962 Gen. Anthis reported that VNAF training was proceeding satisfactorily although there were problems in training inadequately-educated Vietnamese to become pilots, mechanics, and radar specialists. Students had difficulty using the English language properly. It was also troublesome to obtain security clearances quickly for prospective pilots who were scheduled to train in the United States, especially after two dissident VNAF members bombed the government palace in February 1962. Another difficulty concerned some VNAF C-47 pilots who had been trained by the French and were reluctant to change their flying techniques.[6]

In April the VNAF possessed 63 fighters (19 AD-6's and 44 T-28's) and 117 support aircraft (C-47's, L-19/20's, and H-34C's). During the month, LeMay and an Air Staff group inspected the VNAF and found its fighters marginally adequate. The VNAF, the group decided, needed improved planes and more and better trained T-28 pilots. The VNAF commander, a colonel, had too low a rank compared to his ARVN counterpart. The group also supported the desire of the Diem government to obtain jet aircraft.[7]

The three-year comprehensive plan to train and equip the Vietnamese to defend themselves and to phase out major U.S. activities,* proposed by the JCS in July 1962, called for the Vietnamese regular and paramilitary strength to reach a peak of 575,000 in fiscal year 1964 and decline thereafter. The size of the VNAF would reach 16 squadrons (three fighter,

---

*As noted earlier, the JCS integrated this plan with the 1964-1969 military assistance program and the national campaign plan. See p 30.

four transport, one reconnaissance, four liaison, and four helicopter). To modernize the Vietnamese air arm, the United States would provide nonjet A-1H and jet F5A/B fighters and nonjet RT-28 and jet RF-5B reconnaissance aircraft. These planes would be added to the six T/RT-33 jets programmed for delivery which the State Department had not yet approved. Two C-123 squadrons would strengthen VNAF transport capability. In the critical 1964-1965 period, VNAF strength would rise to about 9,000 men.[8]

To enable the VNAF to absorb the new equipment and to reduce language and security problems, PACAF proposed that a larger portion of VNAF training be conducted in South Vietnam. The JCS approved the proposal on 25 April 1963, and Diem heartily endorsed it. (Earlier, the Vietnamese leader had informed Zuckert that 61 percent of VNAF training should be in South Vietnam and only 39 percent in the United States.)[9]

On 6 May McNamara concluded that 1964-1969 MAP funds for South Vietnam would be insufficient to carry out the large contemplated program. Since an F-5 cost about $1 million, he vetoed the proposal to equip the VNAF with it on grounds of cost-effectiveness. A revised program for training more members of the VNAF in South Vietnam was quickly prepared and approved by McNamara on 27 May. It provided for the purchase and deployment of 25 U-17A's plus a USAF detachment to train VNAF personnel in their use. It also augmented a USAF helicopter training detachment that had arrived in South Vietnam in January 1963. By December, when the VNAF had 228 aircraft, the stepped-up training program was well under way.[10]

Meanwhile, on 1 July 1963, the government increased the VNAF personnel authorization from 7,651 to 8,897. In December it possessed 8,496 men: 805 officers, including 376 pilots, and 7,691 enlisted men. Although the Air Force trained most members of the VNAF either in South Vietnam or the United States, the U.S. Army and Navy also gave some assistance. Despite its efforts to make the VNAF operationally self-sufficient, the Air Force expected the shortage of aircraft control and warning, maintenance, and other technical personnel to continue until fiscal year 1965.[11]

The Problem of Jet Aircraft

From 1961 through 1963 Headquarters USAF strongly supported the assignment of jets to the VNAF for use in border surveillance. Assuming that these planes would eventually be authorized, the Air Staff programmed six T/RT-33's for the Vietnamese in the fiscal year 1961 USAF military assistance program.[12]

In October 1961 OSD and the JCS agreed that VNAF jet training was imperative because of the growing Viet Cong threat, the unstable situation in Laos, and the growing obsolescence of the AD-6's. On the 19th, the State Department instructed Ambassador Nolting to inform the Diem government that the United States would train Vietnamese to fly the six T/RT-33's. It asked the government not to publicize the offer until the two countries reached a decision concerning observance of the Geneva agreement which prohibited the use of jets in South Vietnam. After the Vietnamese completed their training, the United States would transfer the jets when it believed that they were needed and the pilots were able to fly them properly.[13]

In July 1962, after training had begun, McNamara questioned whether jets were needed in South Vietnam in place of conventional aircraft. He believed that the time had not yet come to violate the Geneva agreement. The Air Force, Felt, and Harkins urged the transfer of the six aircraft without delay, however.[14]

In January 1963 the JCS also asked McNamara to authorize the transfer of jets, citing his statement of 8 October 1962 that called for a VNAF that could satisfy requirements. The JCS noted that better reconnaissance and other aircraft were needed for stepped up military operations and to counter heavier antiaircraft fire. In addition, there had been no significant political repercussions to the earlier entry of RF-101's and F-102's into South Vietnam. Zuckert endorsed this JCS position.[15]

OSD then decided to favor delivery of the jets, but State Department officials, led by Assistant Secretary Harriman, opposed the move. They argued that USAF pilots were not only better able to fly reconnaissance missions than the Vietnamese but were also subject to U.S. political control. If the VNAF flew jets, they claimed, the war would not be shortened but its terms, as understood by both sides, would change significantly. The International Control Commission and other nations in Southeast Asia would consider VNAF jet operations a violation of the Geneva agreement and a definite escalation of the war.[16]

When McNamara informed Taylor and Zuckert on 17 May of this opposition, he told them that the State Department might reconsider its stand at a later date if circumstances warranted, but he urged both men to take a "hard look" at plans for future jet deliveries to the VNAF. As mentioned earlier,[*] he opposed any plans to equip the VNAF with F-5A's. At the end of May, OSD informed CINCPAC that the T/RT-33's would not be transferred to the VNAF.[17]

Late in 1963, when the Viet Cong stepped up its antiaircraft attacks and inflicted heavy damage, the Air Force thought that the Administration might now permit use of high-performance jet aircraft (B-57's) with combined USAF-VNAF crews. A number of VNAF pilots had completed jet training in T-33's and could be ready to fly higher-performance jets in a relatively short time.[18]

---

[*]See p 65.

VIII. THE OVERTHROW OF THE DIEM GOVERNMENT

In 1963 the "clear and hold" tactics adopted in the struggle against the Viet Cong appeared to be succeeding. At the end of 1962, MAC/V had reported that Vietnamese military units were reaching out from cleared areas and fragmenting enemy sources, and Viet Cong morale was low. According to one estimate, enemy casualties had mounted to an estimated 33,000 during 1962--more than double the 1961 figure--as against 13,000 for the government. Viet Cong desertions and weapon losses had increased while its attacks against the Vietnamese armed forces and populace had declined.[1]

Conflicting Evaluations of the War

Early in 1963, most U.S. officials were optimistic. Gen. Maxwell D. Taylor, who became JCS chairman on 1 October 1962, thought the Vietnamese forces were "on the road to victory." To a high State Department official, they were "beginning to win the war." McNamara observed that the Diem government now recontrolled an additional one-fourth of the population. This gave the government, according to Secretary Rusk, control of 951 villages or about half the total, compared with 8 percent held by the Viet Cong and the remainder uncommitted. Felt noted that Viet Cong attacks had dropped from about 100 weekly for the first half of 1962 to about 50 weekly in January 1963, and he pointed to the construction of about 4,000 strategic hamlets.[2]

The Air Force was less optimistic. Zuckert thought "real progress" had been made, but he saw a long struggle ahead. The Air Staff conceded that enemy casualties were high, but it observed that Viet Cong strength had risen from about 16,000 in January 1962 to 22,000 to 24,000 in December, with about 100,000 additional village and provincial forces and political and propaganda agents. In November 1962 the enemy had mounted battalion-size attacks, and the government had failed to seal the Laotian and Cambodian border against infiltration.* And the Diem regime was weak politically and needed to win the support of the people.[3]

One Air Staff study stressed the political restrictions on USAF activities in South Vietnam which limited its participation largely to building up and training the VNAF. It noted that the U.S. Army efforts to "prove" by tests the Howze Board tactical concepts were preempting the traditional USAF role in close support. The study concluded that if the Army effort were successful, it might have an even greater adverse long-range effect on the future U.S. military posture than on the current war against the Viet Cong.[4]

A second study concluded that the Vietnamese forces were not winning. To improve U.S. military support, this country should dispose of the Army-Air Force doctrinal battle and eliminate all but essential testing.

---

*Despite the increase in border control posts, the enemy continued to infiltrate into South Vietnam. Estimates of their number have varied greatly. A detailed MAC/V study in October 1964 arrived at the following figures: 1957-60, 4,500; 1961, 5,400; 1962, 13,000; 1963, 6,200 (including 580 civilian specialists). The infiltrators were believed to be largely retrained military personnel of South Vietnamese origin. The drop in numbers in 1963 appeared to indicate that the Hanoi government had used most of its South Vietnamese veterans of the French Indochina War and was relying on draftees of North Vietnamese origin.

An air deputy commander in USMAC/V should improve air-ground operations. The United States should deploy more USAF aircraft, step up VNAF training, remove political restrictions against defoliation, and encourage third-country aid, particularly by the Chinese Nationalist Air Force. Finally, there should be more overt and covert strikes against North Vietnam despite the increased risk of military escalation.[5]

U.S. newsmen frequently criticized the war effort also, contrasting the pessimistic reports from lower U.S. echelons with those of top officials. These newsmen believed that the Vietnamese lacked sufficient offensive spirit and that Diem lacked public support and interfered with the military to prevent the rise of a rival leader. So severe were some of these criticisms that Felt, in November 1962, informed OSD that there might be a well-planned "whispering campaign" against military activities in South Vietnam that merited investigation.[6]

A Senate foreign relations subcommittee, headed by Senator Mike Mansfield, visited South Vietnam and, in its report early in 1963, doubted that optimism was justified. It warned that U.S. involvement in lives and resources might reach "a scale which would bear little relationship to the interests of the United States or, indeed, to the interests of the people of South Vietnam."[7]

Notwithstanding the critics, the counsels of optimism continued to prevail. In May 1963 U.S. officials again concluded that most "indicators" of progress--Viet Cong casualties, defections, and fewer attacks--were favorable. The strategic hamlet program showed rapid progress, and the Diem forces would begin to carry out the much-delayed national campaign plan on 1 July. But important problems remained, especially the infiltration of insurgents and the concealed delivery of supplies from Laos and Cambodia. To reduce the flow, U.S. and South Vietnamese officials agreed on 1 May to conduct air and ground operations closer to the border areas than had previously been allowed. In addition, the JCS considered proposals to expand covert military operations against North Vietnam to convince the government of that country that it must stop aiding the Viet Cong or suffer more serious reprisals. Both the Army and CINCPAC prepared specific plans for such operations. LeMay believed that the Army plan of "hit and run" airborne and amphibious raids near the coast line was too restrictive. On 22 May the JCS approved a concept for expanding such covert activities.[8]

Reflecting the general U.S. confidence at the time, McNamara in May asked for a plan to train enough Vietnamese so that about 1,000 U.S. military personnel could return to the United States by the end of 1965. Suggested by the British Advisory Mission to South Vietnam, this action would demonstrate the U.S. intention to withdraw, indicate that Vietnamese forces were winning, and blunt the growing opposition to the Diem government. Headquarters USAF hoped that the withdrawal would reduce the spiraling testing activity in South Vietnam which, it believed, was interfering with the war effort.[9]

The Fall of the Diem Regime

Although optimistic, U.S. officials were aware of the dangers that might result from the political and religious conflicts in South Vietnam.

Ambassador Nolting observed on 6 May 1963 that U.S. relations with the Diem regime had deteriorated because Diem considered our Laos policies equivocal, resented our alleged intrusion in Vietnamese affairs, and believed the Mansfield Report a criticism of his regime. Two days later, Diem's security forces fired into a Buddhist demonstration, killing several people. Subsequently, his regime faced more demonstrations, dramatic protests by self-immolation, and talk of a military coup. To defend itself, it arrested many Vietnamese and in late summer temporarily declared a state of martial law.[10]

Weighing the possibility of a debacle, the services drew up plans for evacuating by air and sea about 4,600 noncombatants. For this eventuality, PACAF placed 46 aircraft, mostly C-130's, on alert in Okinawa in August. The United States continued to back Diem, but President Kennedy on 2 September warned that without public support the Vietnamese government could lose the war. The United States renewed its efforts to persuade Diem to stop oppressing his people, but without success.[11]

Despite the political and religious disorders, U.S. officials up to 1 November 1963 were still optimistic. On 2 October McNamara and Taylor, after visiting South Vietnam, still hoped to withdraw 1,000 U.S. troops by the end of the year and complete most of America's military task by the end of 1965. JCS optimism was based on Vietnamese achievements. About 8,300 strategic hamlets had been built for 9.7 million Vietnamese, and 5,200 village and hamlet radio sets had been installed. Overall Viet Cong strength had decreased from 123,000 in

November 1962 to 93,000 a year later, and about 14,000 insurgents had defected since April 1963. Except for the swampy Mekong delta, the Vietnamese appeared to have made good progress in clearing northern and central areas and in opening roads and rail lines.[12]

On 1 November the political and military situation changed drastically. A military junta, headed my Maj. Gen. Duong Van Minh, overthrew the Diem government and shot both Diem and his brother, Ngo Dinh Nhu, the following morning. On the 5th, the junta formed a civilian provincial government. Military leaders stated that one reason for the coup was their belief that Nhu, Diem's chief political advisor, was negotiating an unacceptable compromise with North Vietnam to settle the war. For political and other reasons, more than 400 Vietnamese officers were soon discharged and others placed on leave without pay.[13]

The "Number One" Problem

Although the political and military situation deteriorated after the coup, the United States announced on 14 November its intention to withdraw as planned about 1,000 troops engaged in engineering, ordnance, medicine, and similar tasks. Beginning 3 December, these troops, which included 274 USAF personnel, departed from South Vietnam.[14]

The political and military setback following the coup did not change basic U.S. policy toward South Vietnam. After conferring with the National Security Council, President Johnson on 26 November asserted that the principal U.S. objective would still be to assist the new government to consolidate itself, win public support, and defeat the Communists. To implement this policy, the United States would attempt to persuade the new government to concentrate its efforts within the Mekong delta. U.S. military planners would consider the possibility of more action against North Vietnam and the Communists in Laos. This country would make a greater effort to improve relations with Cambodia (a Viet Cong sanctuary) and also show the world how the insurgents were controlled and supported by nations outside South Vietnam.[15]

Declaring Vietnam to be the "number one" problem of the United States, President Johnson on 2 December directed the JCS to send only the best U.S. military personnel to that country. By year's end, U.S. and Vietnamese military leaders were preparing a new pacification plan which, they hoped, would reverse the recent tide of defeat.[16]

Meanwhile, as the insurgents continued their offensive, the Administration directed more attention to controlling the flow of men and supplies from Laos and Cambodia. In view of the political obstacles to "hot pursuit" and inspection, especially in Cambodia,* McNamara in January 1964 urged more high and low reconnaissance missions. The JCS desired a still bolder program, recommending that the United States temporarily assume tactical direction of the war and deploy more U.S. forces, including combat units, if necessary. They also suggested that MAC/V be responsible for all U.S. programs in South Vietnam, U.S. pilots overfly Cambodia and Laos, and the South Vietnamese conduct operations against North Vietnam and Laos. Whether any of these recommendations would be adopted in 1964 remained to be seen.[17]

---

*In November 1963 U.S.-Cambodia relations reached a new low when the Cambodian government terminated U.S. economic and military assistance.

IX. SUMMARY, 1961-1963

The growing Communist menace to South Vietnam in 1959-1960 found the U.S. government responding gradually. By late 1961 an initial program of action stressing military training and economic projects was deemed insufficient. As a result, President Kennedy sent his Military Representative, General Taylor, and other U.S. officials to South Vietnam to assess the threat. The Taylor Mission recommended more military and economic aid and greater, although limited, U.S. participation in training, advisory, and support activities. McNamara and the JCS thought that the situation in both South Vietnam and Laos merited the use of SEATO or U.S. combat forces. But fearing military escalation, the Administration generally accepted the Taylor Mission's program.

By late 1961 U.S. military units and advisory and training personnel were deploying to South Vietnam. The Air Force deployed a small special air warfare unit eventually nicknamed Farmgate, one C-123 transport squadron, and other support aircraft and equipment including a tactical air control system. The basic mission of Farmgate was to advise and train the Vietnamese Air Force. Combat training missions with combined USAF-VNAF crews were authorized only when the VNAF was unable to fulfill all air support needs. In February 1962 a U.S. Military Assistance Command, Vietnam, was established in Saigon to coordinate all U.S. activities in support of the Vietnamese.

In mid-1962 initial evaluations of limited "clear and hold" and other support operations were optimistic. In the limited air war, USAF combat training and transport sorties increased, defoliation tests were promising, and USAF strength had been augmented. But the Air Force chafed under the restraints imposed by the Department of State, OSD, and the Army. These restraints limited air strikes for fear they would harm friendly Vietnamese, create undesirable political repercussions, and escalate the war. Equally disturbing to the Air Force was its subordinate military planning role under both CINCPAC and MAC/V, especially the latter. This contributed to Air Force failure to win approval of some of its own concepts for defeating the Viet Cong, such as the quick reaction plan of early 1962. There was also a growing Air Force-Army dispute over tactical air control.

Although Farmgate sorties increased, new air tactics evolved, and Farmgate-VNAF air strikes accounted for a high percent of Viet Cong casualties, the political restrictions on Farmgate activities remained. Air Force-Army differences over the use of airpower in counterinsurgency were intensified as the Army began testing "Howze Board" tactical air concepts that, the Air Force believed, preempted its own long-established tactical roles and missions. The conflict reached the highest OSD level when a strike against the Viet Cong on 2 January 1963 resulted in high losses, allegedly because of inadequate use of air support. A JCS team reviewed the incident, the war's conduct, and Air Force grievances, but the Air Force won only minor concessions. Because of Army or OSD opposition it also failed to obtain the post of chief of staff or to create the post of air deputy commander in MAC/V.

Meanwhile, in late 1962 and early 1963, most top officials remained hopeful about the war's progress on the basis of enemy casualties, defections, reduced terror strikes, and the progress of the Diem government's strategic hamlet program designed to isolate the populace from the Viet Cong. But much of the U.S. news media, pointing to the ineffectiveness of the Diem government and the Vietnamese forces, thought that the optimism was unjustified. A Senate foreign relations subcommittee questioned the wisdom of growing U.S. involvement.

Some Air Force officers who took a somber view thought that the war was being lost. Observing the increasing value of VNAF and Farmgate missions in stopping or deterring Viet Cong attacks against villages, outposts, strategic hamlets, and rail and road convoys; and for inflicting casualties, destroying equipment and supplies, and inhibiting enemy movement, they urged greater use of airpower. They also recommended jet aircraft for both USAF and VNAF units to conduct air strikes more effectively and to counter the effects of increased antiaircraft fire. They urged the removal of political restrictions against border flights, defoliation, and other activities.

In early 1963 U.S. authorities, in the light of growing military requirements, authorized the Air Force and the U.S. Army to augment partially their air strength in Vietnam. This would enhance the mobility of the Vietnamese Army and paramilitary forces, provide additional air support for a national campaign plan designed to shorten the war, and permit the withdrawal of most U.S. units, except training, by the end of 1965. A decision to accelerate the training and equipping of the VNAF added to the Air Force's commitment.

In the spring of 1963, rising religious and political unrest against the Diem regime was highlighted by Buddhist and student demonstrations. As political deterioration continued, U.S. efforts to persuade the regime to be less oppressive were unsuccessful. Most U.S. authorities continued to believe that U.S.-South Vietnamese military operations still presaged success. But the government's unpopularity and the belief that it harbored secret neutralization plans led on 1 November to a military coup d'etat. In subsequent weeks Viet Cong attacks increased to take advantage of the political disorder. The 1st Air Commando Squadron (previously Farmgate) and the VNAF flew large numbers of sorties to aid strategic hamlets overrun or threatened by the Communists.

The immediate post-coup period vitiated much of the previous two-year's military and economic gains and demonstrated the persistent, growing Viet Cong strength. Although programs and tactics were reviewed, there were few indications that U.S. Government policies limiting direct USAF participation, permitting the use of Army tactical air concepts, and encouraging Army aviation testing, would be greatly modified. In fact, personnel changes in MAC/V placed the day-to-day conduct of the war even more firmly in Army hands. In air support the Army's domination was dramatized by the greater number of aircraft on hand and sorties flown compared with the Air Force. However, heavier aircraft attrition from ground fire, McNamara's request for more air reconnaissance of borders, and the slow progress of the VNAF suggested the possible use of more USAF aircraft, including jets.

At the end of 1963 President Johnson asserted that the United States would help the new South Vietnamese government consolidate itself and win the support of the people. Observing that the war was America's "number one" problem, he directed the use of only "blue-ribbon" U.S. military personnel. As a gesture of confidence, 1,000 U.S. officers and men, including 274 from the Air Force, were returned to the United States in December. But as 1964 began the JCS was increasingly apprehensive of Viet Cong strength and advocated stronger U.S. action against border areas and North Vietnam. They urged temporary overall U.S. direction of the war. Whether the political rules of the war would be significantly relaxed as the JCS counseled--and as the Air Force had recommended--remained to be seen.

NOTES

Unless otherwise noted, all primary sources cited (letters, memos, JCS papers) are located in Headquarters USAF Directorate of Plans File RL (61), (62), (63), or (64) 38-9, depending upon the year of the source.

CHAPTER I

1. Bureau Int & Rsch, Dept of State, Summary of Principal Events in History of Vietnam, 10 Jan 62 (hereinafter referred to as RFE-14) in AFCHO; R. W. Lindholm, ed, Vietnam, The First Five Years (Michigan State, 1959), p 4; A. B. Cole, ed, Conflict in Indo-China and International Repercussions, A Documentary History, 1945-1955 (New York, 1956), p 195; J. K. King, Southeast Asia in Perspective (New York, 1956), p 170.

2. RFE-14, 10 Jan 62.

3. Cole, pp 195 and 255; British Information Service, Vietnam (London, 1961), p 18.

4. See note above; King, p 171; Robert Scigliano, South Vietnam, Nation Under Stress (Boston, 1963), pp 162-63.

5. Cole, pp 195, 255; King, p 171; Scigliano, pp 162-63; British Info Svc, Vietnam, pp 14-15; House Hearings before Subcmte on Far East and Pacific of Cmte on Foreign Affairs, 27 Jul-15 Aug 59, Current Situation in the Far East, p 35.

6. Capt Mack D. Secord, "The Viet Nam Air Force," Air University Review, Nov-Dec 63, p 60; Journal of Mutual Security (JMS), prep by Asst for Mutual Security, May 57, pp 154-55, p 126, and Mar 59, p 149.

7. Cole, pp 251-56; RFE-14, 10 Jan 62; British Info Svc, Vietnam, p 15; Bernard F. Fall, The Two Vietnams, A Political and Military Analysis (New York, 1963), p 219.

8. JMS, Nov 60, p 35; British Info Svc, Vietnam, p 14.

9. Scigliano, pp 138, 163-64; Secord, p 60; JMS, May 57, pp 154-55, Mar 58, p 126, and Mar 59, p 149.

10. Dept of State, Vietnam: Guidelines for Policy and Operations, Feb 63, p 19; RAND RM-4140 PR, Jul 64, The Role of North Vietnam in the Southern Insurgency, pp 31-36.

11. Ltr, CINCPAC to JCS, 27 Mar 61, subj: SVN Internal Security Situation, 1960; Dept of State Press Release 287, 4 May 61.

Notes to Page 6 - 11

12. Memo, Dep D/Plans for Policy to C/S USAF, 3 Nov 61, subj: Background Paper on CINCPAC Oplan 32-59; Hist, CINCPAC, 1961, pt 1, pp 168-69.

13. Ltr, CINCPAC to JCS, 18 Jan 61, subj: Increased Force Levels for RVN Armed Forces; memo, P. M. Nitze, Asst SOD/ISA to Chmn JCS, 25 Jan 61, subj: U.S. Support for Addit Mil Forces in VN and Thai; memo, SOD to Secy State, 30 Jan 61, no subj; rpt, VN: Dept of State Guidelines for Policy and Ops, Apr 62; JCS 1992/917, 9 Feb 61; Hist, CINCPAC, 1961, pt 1, pp 169-70.

14. Memo, M/G D. A. Burchinal, D/Plans to C/S USAF, 20 Jun 61, subj: Increase in GVN Forces.

15. Ltr, CINCPAC to JCS, 27 Mar 61, subj: SVN Internal Security Sit, 1960; JCS 2343/21/1, 8 Nov 61; Hist, CINCPAC, 1961, pt 1, pp 169-70.

16. Memo, Col A. N. Williams, Dep D/Plans for Policy to C/S USAF, 9 May 61, subj: Prog of Action for VN; Hist, CINCPAC, 1961, pt 1, p 172; rpt, Prog of Action to Prevent Communist Domination of SVN, 6 May 61; NSA memo 52, 11 May 61.

17. See note above; Dept of State rsch memo, RFE-14, 10 Jan 62.

18. Memo, SAF to SOD, 9 May 61, subj: Prog of Action for VN, in OSAF 1257-61; memo, Burchinal to C/S USAF, 17 May 61, same subj.

19. JCS 2343/1, 7 Jul 61; JCS 2343/67, 13 Jan 62; rpt, Jt Action Prog Proposed by the VN-US Spec Financial Gps . . . to Pres Diem and Kennedy, Jul 61; ltr, CINCPAC to JCS, 9 Jun 61, subj: Increase in Force Level for RVN; memo, Burchinal to C/S USAF, 20 Jun 61, subj: Increase in GVN Forces; ltr, Actg SOD to Secy State, 3 Jul 61, no subj; JCS 2343/5, 26 Jul 61; NSA memo 65, 11 Aug 61.

20. NSA memo 65, 11 Aug 61; memo, SOD to Chmn JCS, 5 Feb 62, subj: Increase of all GVN Forces; JCS 2343/67, 13 Jan 62; memo, Dep SOD to SA, et al., 18 Aug 61, subj: Joint Prog of Action by GVN, in OSAF 1257-61.

21. JCS 2343/25, 9 Oct 61; memo, Dep SOD to Chmn JCS, 5 Oct 61, subj: Concept For Use of SEATO Forces in VN; memo, SOD to SA, et al., 21 Oct 61, subj: SEA; New York Times, 12 Oct 61; Public Papers of the Presidents of the United States, John F. Kennedy . . . 1961 (GPO, 1962), pp 680-81; Dept of Defense Annual Report for Fiscal Year 1963, p 192; New York Times, 2 Jul 63.

22. Msg 38287, CINCPAC to JCS, 24 Oct 61; ltr, Gen Maxwell D. Taylor, Mil Rep Pres, to Pres, 3 Nov 61, no subj, with atchd rpt on Gen Taylor's Mission to SVN and anx A through I.

23. Draft memo, SOD to Pres, 6 Nov 61, no subj; JCS 2343/36, 9 Nov 61.

Notes to Pages 12 - 17   83

24. JCS 2343/40, 13 Nov 61; memo, M/G J. W. Carpenter, III, Dep D/Plans, to C/S USAF, 13 Nov 61, subj: SVN; memo, Burchinal to C/S USAF, 20 Nov 61.

25. NSA memo 111, 22 Nov 61; Dept of State Bul, 4 Dec 61, pp 920-21.

26. NSA memo 111, 22 Nov 61; rpt, Vietnam: Dept of State Guidelines for Policy and Ops, Apr 62; Dept of State Press Release 8, 4 Jan 62; Dept of State Pub 7308, 8 Dec 61, A Threat to the Peace: North Vietnam's Efforts to Conquer South Vietnam, pts 1 and 2.

27. Memo, C/S USAF to JCS, 5 Dec 61, subj: SVN; JCS 2343/70, 13 Jan 62; memo, SOD to Pres, no subj, 27 Jan 62.

CHAPTER II

1. Memo, B/G G. S. Brown, Mil Asst to SOD to SA, et al., 27 Nov 61, subj: SVN; memo, SOD to JCS, 27 Nov 61, subj: First Phase of the VN Prog; memo, SOD to Pres, 22 Dec 61, subj: Mil Cmd in SVN; memo, L/Col S.B. Berry, Jr., Mil Asst to SOD to SA, et al., 4 Dec 61; Dept of State Bul, 4 Dec 61, pp 920-21.

2. Memo, Dep SOD to Chmn JCS, et al., 4 Jan 62, subj: Pub Affairs Security Aspects of Ops in VN.

3. JCS, 2343/46, 22 Nov 61.

4. Memo, Asst SOD/ISA to SOD, 1 Dec 61, subj: VN Comd Arrangements; ltr, Secy State to SOD, 18 Dec 61, no subj.

5. Ibid; ltr, SOD to Secy State, 7 Dec 61, no subj; memo, SOD to Pres, 22 Dec 61, no subj; Baltimore Sun, 9 Feb 62.

6. Memo, SOD to Pres, 22 Dec 61, no subj; JCS 2343/62, 8 Feb 62; ltr, Pres to all Ambassadors, 29 May 61; msg 2393, JCS to CINCPAC, 28 Nov 61; msg 01600, CINCPAC to CNO, et al., 8 Feb 62, in Hist Study, Contemporary Historical Evaluation of Counterinsurgency Operations, Oct 1961-Dec 1963 (hereinafter cited as Project CHECO SEA Rpt), prep by Hq PACAF (May 1964), pt IV-A, docs 1 and 8; DOD Press Release 204-62, 8 Feb 62.

7. Memo, Carpenter to C/S USAF, 17 Sep 63, subj: Proposed Change in Service Manning in C/S Position, USMAC/V; msg 28784, PACAF to C/S USAF, 8 Dec 61; msg, PACAF to C/S USAF, 13 Dec 61; msg 43936, PACAF to C/S USAF, 18 Feb 62; msg 63603, Hq USAF to PACAF, 21 Feb 62.

8. Memo, Carpenter to C/S USAF, 17 Sep 63; rpt, C/S Visit to SVN, 24 Apr 62; memo, Col F. R. Pancake, Asst Dep D/Plans to C/S USAF, 5 Jan 63, subj: Review of Mil Sit in SVN; msg 43936, PACAF to C/S USAF, 18 Feb 62.

Notes to pages 17 - 22

9. Msg 020145, CINCPAC to JCS, 2 Nov 61; msg 072013, CINCPAC to Ch USMAAG/V, 7 Nov 61; msg 252015A, CINCPAC to Ch MAAG/V, 25 Nov 61; msg 16790, PACAF to C/S USAF, 29 Nov 61.

10. Hist, 2d ADVON, 15 Nov 61-8 Oct 62, pp xviii, 17; JCS 2343/191, 4 Feb 63.

11. Memo, SOD to SA, et al., 21 Oct 61, subj: SEA; memo, Brown to SA, et al., 27 Nov 61, subj: SVN; Charles H. Hildreth, USAF Counterinsurgency Doctrines and Capabilities, 1961-1962 (AFCHO, 1964), pp 12-14, in AFCHO; Hist, PACAF, Jul-Dec 61, I, pt 2, p 23.

12. Msg 25979, JCS to CINCPAC, 6 Dec 61; msg 44865, JCS to CINCPAC, 26 Dec 61; msg 41464, CINCPAC to PACAF, 20 Dec 61; memo, L/Col J.B. Owens, Combined Plans Div, D/Plans, to C/S USAF, 13 Feb 62, subj: Actions Concerning SVN; Hist, CINCPAC, 1961, pt 1, pp 187-88; Rcrd, SOD Honolulu Conference (hereinafter referred to as Hono Conf), 16 Dec 61, in AFCHO.

13. Hist, PACAF, Jul-Dec 61, I, pt 2, pp 19-20.

14. Ibid.; Hist, 13th AF, Jul-Dec 61, pp 62-70.

15. Hist, 13th AF, Jul-Dec 61, p 86; Hist, PACAF, Jul-Dec 62, I, pt 2, pp 27-28; Rcrd, SOD Hono Conf, 19 Feb 62.

16. Rcrd, SOD Hono Conf, 15 Jan 62 and 19 Feb 62; Hist, PACAF, Jul-Dec 61, I, pt 2, p 28; Hist, 13th AF, Jul-Dec 61, p 86.

17. Memo, Col R. P. Baldwin, Air Def Dev, D/Ops to Engr Div, D/Ops, 28 Nov 61, subj: Talking Paper--TAC Control Capability; Hist, CINCPAC, 1961, pt 1, pp 33, 175; Hist, 2d ADVON, 15 Nov 61-8 Oct 62, p 10.

18. Rcrd, SOD Hono Conf, 16 Dec 61 and 15 Jan 62; Hist, 2d ADVON, 15 Nov 61-8 Oct 62, pp 91-93.

19. Rcrd, SOD Hono Conf, 16 Jan 62; Hist, CINCPAC, 1962, p 164; Hist, D/Ops, Jan-Jun 62, pp 57-58; Hist, 2d ADVON, 15 Nov 61-8 Oct 62, p 95 and app D, item 21; "Tactical Air Control in the VNAF," Air University Review, Sep-Oct 63, pp 75-81, prep by AU Rev staff.

21. JCS 2343/68, 9 Jan 62; memo, Dep SOD to SA, et al., 13 Jan 62; Rcrd, SOD Hono Conf, 15 Jan 62; Hist, D/Telecom, Jul-Dec 62, pp 108-09; Hist, AFLC, 1 Jul 62-30 Jun 63, pt II, pp 53-57.

CHAPTER III

1. Rcrd, SOD Hono Conf, 16 Dec 61, item 4.

2. Ibid., 15 Jan 62, item 6.

Notes to Pages 23 - 26

3. Memo, Carpenter to C/S USAF, 22 Mar 62, subj: Buildup in SVN, 6 Dec 61; memo, C/S USAF to SOD, 4 Apr 62, subj: Estab of Quick Reaction Forces in SVN; memo, Chmn JCS to SOD, 17 Nov 62, subj: Viet Cong Attacks on Strat Hamlets; rpt, C/S USAF Visit to SVN, 16-21 Apr 62, prep by D/Plans, 24 Apr 62 (hereinafter cited as LeMay Rpt); Hist, CINCPAC, 1962, p 179.

4. See note above; draft memo by C/S Army, 1 Mar 62, subj: Estab of Quick Reaction Forces in SVN; msg 85592, Hq USAF to PACAF, 5 May 62; msg 67265, Hq USAF to PACAF, 18 Jul 62; Hildreth, Counterinsurgency, 1961-1962, pp 24-25.

5. Memo, SAF to SOD, 4 Dec 61, no subj, in OSAF 1257-61; memo, Dep SOD to Chmn JCS, et al., 4 Jan 62, subj: Pub Affairs and Security Aspects of Ops in VN; Rcrd, SOD Hono Conf, 19 Feb 62, p 33.

6. Memo, Owens to C/S USAF, 13 Feb 62, subj: Actions Concerning SVN; Rcrd, SOD Hono Conf, 15 Jan 62, pp 3-1 to 3-5; JCS 2343/96, 19 Mar 62; Hist, PACAF, Jul-Dec 61, pt 2, pp 23-28.

7. Hist, 2d ADVON, 15 Nov 61-8 Oct 62, pp 127-30.

8. Ibid, p 133; memo, M/G R. F. Worden, Dep D/Plans, to C/S USAF, 23 Jan 64, subj: JCS Briefing by Gen Anthis.

9. Rcrd, SOD Hono Conf, 19 Feb 62, pp 15-16; LeMay Rpt, 24 Apr 62; L/Col E. T. Cragg, Asst Dep D/War Plans, D/Plans, to C/S USAF, 2 Mar 62, subj: Actions Concerning SVN; memo for rcrd by M. C. Loughlin, Cold War Div, D/Plans, 12 Mar 62, no subj; msg 38634, PACAF to C/S USAF, 4 Apr 62; New York Times, 19 Feb 62; msg 67718, Hq USAF to PACAF, 8 Mar 62, in Project CHECO SEA Rpt, pt V-A, doc no 60; and pt III, pp 26-27.

10. Hist, 2d ADVON, 15 Nov 61-8 Oct 62, p 133; New York Times, 27 Mar 62; Baltimore Sun, 12 Jul 62.

11. Memo, M/G W. W. Momyer, D/Ops Rqts to DCS/O, 3 Apr 62, subj: Suspected Communist Night Air Activity in SVN; Hist, CINCPAC, 1962, pp 188-89; Hist, 13th AF, pp 75, 81-82; LeMay Rpt, 24 Apr 62; JMS, Mar 62, p 171; Washington Post, 3 Apr 62.

12. Rcrd, SOD Hono Conf, 19 Feb 62; memo, M/G S. W. Agee, D/Ops, to Under SAF, 20 Mar 62, subj: Ranch Hand; Hist, CINCPAC, 1962, pp 187-88; Hist of Airlift in SVN, Dec 61-Oct 62, prep by 6492d Combat Cargo Gp (P), 17 Dec 62, pp 15, 18-19, in AFCHO; Hildreth, USAF Special Air Warfare Doctrines and Capabilities, 1963 (AFCHO, 1964), p 32, in AFCHO.

13. Msg 25786, PACAF to Hq USAF, 13 Mar 62; Hist, 13th AF, 1962, p 63.

14. Rcrd, SOD Hono Conf, 16 Dec 61, item 2; memo, R/Adm J. H. Wellings, Vice D/Joint Staff to Asst to SOD Spec Ops, 3 Feb 62, subj: Bien Hoa Ops of 21 Jan 62; memo for rcrd by Owens, 7 Feb 62, subj: Bien Hoa Cambodian Village Incident.

15. See note above; ltr, U. Alexis Johnson, Dep Under Secy of State to W. P. Bundy, Asst SOD/ISA, 24 Jan 62, no subj; memo, Chmn JCS to SOD, 30 Jan 62, no subj; msg 36258, PACAF to C/S USAF, 12 Feb 62.

16. Msg 36257, PACAF to C/S USAF, 12 Feb 63; msg 36121, PACAF to C/S USAF, 12 Feb 61; msg 36122, PACAF to C/S USAF, 13 Feb 62; Rcrd, SOD Hono Conf, 19 Feb 62, item 5.

17. Msg 14539, PACAF to USAF, 16 Mar 62; Hist, 2d ADVON, 15 Nov 61-8 Oct 62, pp 162-64; msg 1173, Dept of State to AmEmb Saigon, 4 Apr 62; New York Times, 16 Mar 62; New York Herald Tribune, 25 Mar 62.

18. LeMay Rpt, 24 Apr 62.

CHAPTER IV

1. Rcrd, SOD Hono Conf, 11 May and 23 Jul 62; rpt, Visit to SEA by SOD, 8-11 May 62, Ch III, pp 1-3; New York Times, 12 May 62; Philadelphia Inquirer, 22 May 62; New York News, 2 Jun 62; Baltimore Sun, 12 Jul 62; rpt, OSI to IG Hq USAF, Jun 63, subj: Viet Cong, in OSAF 290-63.

2. Rcrd, SOD Hono Conf, 23 Jul and 8 Oct 62; memo, V. H. Krulak, Off of Spec Asst for COIN and Spec Activities, OSD to C/S Army, et al., 29 Nov 62, subj: Three-Year Prog for U.S. Mil Pers and Materiel Sup for SVN; JCS 2343/119, 4 Feb 63.

3. Rcrd, SOD Hono Conf, 23 Jul 62, pp 7-1 to 7-2.

4. Memo, SOD to Chmn JCS, 23 Aug 62, subj: Three-Year Prog for U.S. Mil Personnel and Materiel Sup for SVN.

5. JCS 2343/191, 4 Feb 63; Rcrd, Discussions on VN at PACOM Hq, Dec 17-18, 1962, pp 5-9; Hist, 2d ADVON, 15 Nov 61-8 Oct 62, app D, item 18.

6. Rcrd, Discussions on VN at PACOM Hq, Dec 17-18, 1962, pp 5-9; msg 11889, PACAF to C/S USAF, 28 Dec 62.

7. JCS 2343/191, 4 Feb 63; memo, B/G G. C. Kelleher, Asst C/S J-3 MAC/V to Senior Advisors in I, II, III, and IV Corps, 21 Feb 63, subj: NCP.

8. Msg 52507, PACAF to C/S USAF, 8 Dec 63; msg 060737, AmEmb Saigon to DOD, et al., 6 Jul 63; Hist, 2d ADVON, 15 Nov 61-8 Oct 62, app D, item 18.

Notes to Pages 32 - 35

9. Msg 060837, AmEmb Saigon to DOD, et al., 6 Jul 63; msg 32186, PACAF to C/S USAF, 10 Jul 63; msg 39276, PACAF to C/S USAF, 30 Aug 63.

10. Msg 69799, Hq USAF to PACAF, 15 Mar 62; msg 16838, PACAF to Hq USAF, 17 Mar 62; JCS 2343/128, 16 Jul 62; Hist, 2d ADVON, 15 Nov 61-8 Oct 62, pp 153-55; Hist, AFLC, 1 Jul 62-30 Jun 63, p 26; Rcrd, SOD Hono Conf, 8 Oct 62, p 5; JCS J-3 Ops 200-62-2, 20 Nov 62; JCS 2343/175, 4 Dec 62; Hist, D/Ops, Jan-Jun 63, pp 64-65; memo, Dep SOD to Chmn JCS, 31 Dec 62.

11. Memos, Carpenter, D/Plans, to C/S USAF, 7 Feb 63 and 28 Feb 63, subj: Air Aug, SVN; Army Staff memo 36-63 to D/Jt Staff, 27 Feb 63; JCS 2343/202, 28 Feb 63; Hist, CINCPAC, 1963, p 213; Hist, D/Ops, Jul-Dec 63, Sec V, p 3; Hist, D/Aerospace Progs, Jan-Jun 63, p 25; Hildreth, Special Air Warfare, 1963, pp 30-32.

12. Talking Paper for Chmn JCS for SOD Mtg, 18 Feb 63; memo, Worden to C/S USAF, 30 Nov 63, subj: Mil Sit in RVN; JCS 2343/21, 25 Mar 63; Rcrd, SOD Hono Conf, 6 May 63; Hist, D/Ops, Jan-Jun 63, pp 54-55; Hist, 13th AF, Jan-Jun 63, pp 72-73; msg 58388, PACAF to C/S USAF, 21 Mar 63.

13. Memo, C/S USAF to JCS, 8 Apr 63, subj: PCS Tsfr of USAF Forces.

14. Ltr, DAF to PACAF, 17 Jun 63, subj: Activation of the 1st Air Commando Sq (C) and Certain Other USAF Unit Actions, in AFCHO; Hist, TAC, Jan-Jun 63, p 71; Hist, D/Ops, Jul-Dec 63, Sec V, p 3; Hist, D/Aerospace Progs, Jan-Jun 63, p 25.

15. Hist, 2d ADVON, 15 Nov 61-8 Oct 62, pp 153-55.

16. Msg 8518, PACAF to C/S USAF, 20 Sep 62; ltr, LeMay to O'Donnell, 1 Sep 62, no subj; Proj CHECO SEA Rpt, pt V, pp 51-55; Hist, 2d ADVON, 15 Nov 61-8 Oct 62, pp 146-50; Excerpt, SAF testimony before House Cmte on Armed Services, 21 Feb 63, in SAFOI.

17. Hist, 2d ADVON, 15 Nov 61-8 Oct 62, pp 146, 150-51; msg 55773, PACAF to C/S USAF, 11 Sep 62; msg 1975, PACAF to C/S USAF, 15 Sep 62.

18. Hist, D/Ops, Jan-Jun 62, pp 47-48; JCS 2343/135, 8 Aug 62; memo, Carpenter to C/S USAF, 3 Aug 62, subj: Decca Navig Sys for SVN; memo, SAF to U. Alexis Johnson, Dep Under Secy State for Pol Affairs, 28 Jan 63, no subj, in OSAF 290-63; ltr, SAF to Sen John Stennis, Chmn Subcmte on Prepared Invest Cmte on Armed Services, 16 Jul 64, no subj, in OSAF 101-64; msg 73737, Hq USAF to AFLC, et al., 10 Aug 62; Hist, D/Maint-Engr, Jul-Dec 62, p 53; Hist, AFLC, 1 Jul 62-30 Jun 63, pt II, pp 45-52.

19. Hist, 2d ADVON, 15 Nov 61-8 Oct 62, p 133; Talking Papers on msg, Dept of State to AmEmb Saigon (Harriman to Nolting), Mar 63; see app 1, 2, 3, and 4.

20. Hist, 2d ADVON, 15 Nov 61-8 Oct 62, p 133, DOD Press Release 16-23, 5 Jan 63; see app 5 and 6.

21. Hist, TAC, Jan-Jun 63, pp 586-87; Talking Papers on msg, Dept of State to AmEmb Saigon, Mar 63; msg, COMUSMAC/V to JCS, et al., 10 Jan 63; see app 2.

22. See note above.

23. Memo, JCS 2343/221, 25 Mar 63; memo, Worden to C/S USAF, 30 Nov 63, subj: Mil Sit in RVN; Talking Paper for Chmn JCS for SOD Mtg, 18 Feb 63; Rcrd, SOD Hono Conf, 6 May 63, pp 1-a-1 to 1-2-6; Hist, D/Ops, Jan-Jun 63, pp 54-66; Hist, 13th AF, Jan-Jun 63, pp 72-73; msg 58388, PACAF to C/S USAF, 21 Mar 63.

24. Msg 94957, C/S USAF to PACAF, 19 Apr 63; msg, PACAF to C/S USAF, 4 Apr 63; Rcrd, SOD Hono Conf, 6 May 63, pp 1-a-5 to 1-a-6; msg 7467, PACAF to C/S USAF, 8 May 63; Hist, TAC, Jan-Jun 63, pp 432, 594-95; memo, T. L. Hughes, Bur Int & Rsch, Dept of State to Secy State, 22 Oct 63, subj: Statistics on War Effort Show Unfavorable Trend; Proj CHECO SEA Rpt, pt VI, pp 54-55.

25. Msg 82504, C/S USAF to PACAF, TAC, 27 Jul 63, doc 60 in Proj CHECO SEA Rpt, Oct 61-Dec 63, Vol V-A.

26. Senate Hearings before Subcmte on DOD Appropriations, 88th Cong, 2d Sess, DOD Appropriations for 1965, pt 1, pp 14-15; Rcrd, SOD Hono Conf, 20 Nov 63; msg 020459, COMUSMAC/V to JCS, 3 Jan 64; msg 080320, COMUSMAC/V to JCS et al, 8 Nov 63, and other weekly COMUSMAC/V "Headway" rpts, Nov-Dec 63; msg 180120, CINCPAC to COMUSMAC/V, 1 Feb 64; ltr, SAF to Sen John Stennis, 16 Jul 64; New York Times, 10 and 23 Dec 63; Washington Post, 14 Nov 63.

27. Ltr, SAF to Rep Carl Vinson, Chmn Cmte on Armed Services, 13 May 64, no subj, in OSAF 101-64; Memo for Rcrd by L/Col W. T. Galligan, Dep Ch, Cong Invest Div, SAFLL, 24 Jun 64, subj: Hearings by Senate Preparedness Invest Subcmte, Senate Cmte on Armed Services, in OSAF 101-64; see app 1, 2, 3, 4, and 5.

28. Msg 132015, COMUSMAC/V to JCS, et al., 13 Jun 63; rpt, AF Study Gp on VN, prep by OSAF, May 64, pt III; msg 290724, COMUSMAC/V to JCS, et al., 29 Nov 63; memo for rcrd, L/Col J. L. Crego, Off D/Plans, 16 Jan 64, no subj; Talking Paper on USAF/U.S. Army a/c Losses and Damages in VN, 17 Jan 64, in OSAF 101-64; see app 7.

29. Hist, D/Ops, Jan-Jun 64, pp 35-40; Hist, 2d AD, Ch I, Jan-Jun 64, pp 45-51; memo, T. D. McKiernan, Asst Dep D/Plans for Policy, D/Plans, to AFCHO, 3 May 65, subj: Draft Study of AFCHO Hist Study, in AFCHO.

Notes to Pages 39 - 45

CHAPTER V

1. DOD Press Release 16-63, 5 Jan 63; <u>Washington Star</u>, 6 Jan 63; <u>Washington Post</u>, 6 Jan 63; JCS 2343/191, 4 Feb 63; Proj CHECO SEA Rpt, pp 89-96.

2. Intvw, author with Col W.V. McBride, Ch Sp Warfare Div, DCS/P&O, 9 Jan 64; JCS 2343/191, 4 Feb 63.

3. Briefing Paper, 11 Jan 63, subj: Air Force Briefing for Gen Wheeler and Others, in Sp Warfare Div, DCS/P&P; Hildreth, <u>Counterinsurgency, 1961-1962</u>, pp 25-36.

4. JCS 2343/191, 4 Feb 63.

5. Rpt, 11 Feb 63, subj: Air Staff Observations During Trip to SVN, prep by L/G D. A. Burchinal, DCS/P&P.

6. Intvw, author with McBride, 9 Jan 64 and 4 Aug 64; Hist, D/Plans, Jan-Jun 63, p 43.

7. Msg, Dept of State to AmEmb Saigon, 22 Mar 63; memo, L/Col A. T. Sampson, Sp Warfare Div, D/Plans, to C/S USAF, 25 Mar 63, subj: State Msg From Nolting, From Mr. Harriman, in Cold War Div, D/Plans.

8. Memo, Pancake to Carpenter, 14 May 63, subj: Value of Interdiction Sorties in SVN.

9. <u>Ibid</u>.; Rcrd, SOD Hono Conf, 6 May 63.

10. Memo, Pancake to Carpenter, 14 May 63; Rcrd, SOD Hono Conf, 6 May 64.

11. Msg 37967, PACAF to C/S USAF, 9 Jul 62, msg 68086, Hq USAF to PACAF, 20 Jul 62; memo, Col L. H. Richmond, Dep D/Plans for War Plans to Cold War Div, D/Plans, 21 Nov 62, subj: Rules of Engagement for Air Ops in SVN; msg 16838, PACAF to Hq USAF, 17 Mar 62; msg 38569, PACAF to C/S USAF, 4 Jul 62; JCS 2343/128, 16 Jul 62.

12. Msg 59249, PACAF to USAF, 3 Mar 62; msg 66331, Hq USAF to PACAF, 5 Mar 62; msg 14539, PACAF to USAF, 16 Mar 62; LeMay Rpt, 24 Apr 62; DOD Press Release 16-23, 5 Jan 63; see app 6.

13. Memo, L/G G. P. Disosway, DCS/O and Momyer, D/Ops Rqts, to C/S USAF, 22 Dec 62, subj: Trip Rpt to SVN (hereinafter cited as Disosway Rpt), in OSAF 11-62; Proj CHECO SEA Rpt, pt V, pp 93-94; Intvw with McBride, 4 Aug 64.

14. Proj CHECO SEA Rpt, pt V, pp 17-18; pt 1, pp 60-61.

15. Memo, Col C. C. Wooten, Ch Spec Advsy Gp, Off Asst C/S Intel to Asst C/S Intel, 7 Nov 62, subj: The Role of Intel in COIN Ops.

16. Memo, Richmond to D/Plans, 21 Nov 62, subj: Rules of Engagement; memo, Worden to C/S USAF, 30 Nov 63, subj: Mil Sit in RVN; Proj CHECO SEA Rpt, pt V, pp 6-10 and pt II, pp 67-91; msg 170525, COMUSMAC/V to JCS 924, 17 Jan 64.

17. Hist, D/Telecom, Jul-Dec 62, p 108; Hist, D/Plans, Jan-Jun 63, pp 242-43; Hist, D/Maint-Engr, Jan-Jun 63, p 71; Proj CHECO SEA Rpt, pt VI, pp 46-49; memo, Worden to C/S USAF, 23 Jan 64, subj: JCS Briefing by Anthis.

18. Proj CHECO SEA Rpt, pt VI, pp 13-17.

19. Ibid., pt IV, pp 38-39; app 6.

20. Msg 2204, JCS to CINCPAC, 23 Apr 62.

21. Msg, CINCPAC to JCS, 26 Apr 62; msg, CINCPAC to Actg Chmn JCS, 27 Apr 62.

22. Msg 56208, PACAF to C/S USAF, 24 Jul 62; msg 19949, PACAF to C/S USAF, 11 Aug 62; msg 36161, PACAF to C/S USAF, 25 Aug 62; Disosway Rpt, 22 Dec 62.

23. Hist, CINCPAC, 1963, p 133; msg 19949, CINCPAC to JCS, 11 Aug 62; msg 88023, C/S USAF to PACAF, 4 Oct 62; Hist, D/Plans, Jan-Jun 63, pp 43, 180; Proj CHECO SEA Rpt, pt IV, pp 41-42.

24. JCS 2428/240-1, 7 Nov 63; memo, Pres to Chmn JCS, 2 Dec 63, no subj; memo, SOD to SA, 6 May 64, no subj; Hist, D/Plans, Jul-Dec 63, p 233; msg 83999, C/S USAF to PACAF, 11 Jan 64.

25. Memo, Carpenter to C/S USAF, Apr 64, subj: Svc Resp for Manning Posn of C/S USMAC/V; Chart, dtd 1961-64 /on Manpower Auth in SVN/, in Off of D/M&O, DCS/P&P; see app 8.

CHAPTER VI

1. Hist, CINCPAC, 1961, pt 1, pp 167, 183.

2. Memo, SOD to Secys of Mil Depts, et al., 5 Sep 61, subj: Exper Comd for Sublimited War, in OSAF; Rcrd, SOD Hono Conf, 16 Jan 62, item 15.

3. Msg 63306, Hq USAF to PACAF, 21 Feb 62; memo, Burchinal to C/S USAF, 8 Jun 62, subj: SOD/JCS Weekly Intel/Ops Briefing, SVN (Project Headway); msg 67265, Hq USAF to PACAF, 18 Jul 62; JCS 2343/131, 18 Jul 62; msg 68501, Hq USAF to PACAF, TAC, AFSC, 23 Jul 62; JCS 2343/129, 28 Jul 62; memo, JCS to SOD, no subj.

4. Msg 78216, Hq USAF to PACAF, 28 Aug 62; JCS 2343/190, 12 Feb 63; JCS Team Trip to SVN, 4 Mar 63; memo, Brown to Dep SOD, 16 Jan 63, subj: Equip Testing in SVN, in OSAF 290-63; Hist, CINCPAC, 1962, pp 168-69.

Notes to Pages 50 – 55

5. Msg 83087, C/S USAF to PACAF, 15 Sep 62; msg 83574, C/S USAF to PACAF, 18 Sep 62; memo, C/S USAF to JCS, 28 Sep 62, subj: Estab of Army Test Unit, VN; msg 89547, C/S USAF to TAC, 10 Oct 62.

6. Msg 46129, PACAF to C/S USAF, 17 Oct 62; Study, Sit in SVN, 17 Dec 62; msg 94785, Hq USAF to PACAF, 7 Nov 62; msg 94853, Hq USAF to TAC, 7 Nov 62; memo, Worden to C/S USAF, 17 Dec 62, subj: Sit in SVN; JCS 2343/203, 4 Mar 63; msg 66967, C/S USAF to PACAF, 9 Jan 63; msg 97337, C/S USAF to PACAF, et al., 23 Nov 62.

7. Memo for Rcrd by L/Col H. M. Chapman, Combined Plans Div, D/Plans, 19 Nov 62, subj: Army Test Unit; JCS 2343/190, 12 Feb 63.

8. JCS 2343/203, 4 Mar 63.

9. Memo, C/S USAF to JCS, 21 Aug 63, subj: Test Plan Air Assault Task Force; memo, C/S USAF to JCS, 23 Oct 63, subj: Serv Test Prog in SVN; memo, Pancake to C/S USAF, 5 Jan 63, subj: Review of Mil Sit in SVN; Burchinal Rpt, 11 Feb 63.

10. JCS 2343/203, 4 Mar 63; memo, Chmn JCS to SOD, 11 Apr 63; subj: R&D Comd Relations; memo, SOD to JCS, 23 Apr 63, same subj.

11. Memo, Carpenter to C/S USAF, 6 Feb 64, subj: Mtg with DDR&E and D/O&MP, OSD; Hist, CINCPAC, 1963, pp 223-24.

12. See note above.

13. Burchinal Rpt, 11 Feb 63; Study, Sit in SVN, 17 Dec 62.

14. Memo, Col A. S. Pouliot, Off D/Ops to C/S USAF, 21 Oct 63, subj: Results of the Employment of OV-1 Mohawk . . . in Support of COIN Ops.

15. Burchinal Rpt, 11 Feb 63; House Hearings before Subcmte on Appropriations, DOD Appropriations for 1964, pt 2, pp 485, 494-95; Senate Hearings before Armed Services Cmte, 88th Cong, 1st Sess, Military Procurement Authorization, FY 1964, pp 314-15.

16. Ltr, JOEG/V-ARPA Field Unit to CINCPAC, 25 Jul 63, subj: JOEG/V's Eval of Armed Helicopters; 1st Ind, Hq USMAC/V, 16 Aug 63, same subj; 2d Ind CINCPAC to JCS, 25 Sep 63, same subj; JCS 2343/270-1, 27 Nov 63.

17. Ltr, JOEG/V-ARPA Field Unit to C/S Army thru CINCPAC, 7 Dec 63, subj: Employment of CU-2B Caribou . . . in Support of COIN Ops.

18. Final Rpt, Opl Test and Eval, YC-123H in RVN, 1 Jun 63, prep by Hq 2d AD, in Hist, 13th AF, Jul-Dec 63, Vol III; memo, JOEG/V-ARPA Field Unit thru COMUSMAC/V to C/S USAF, 26 Aug 63, subj: 2d AD Test and Eval of YC-123H in RVN.

19. Final Rpt, Opl Test and Eval, U-10 in RVN, prep by 2d AD, 1 Jun 63, in Hist, 13th AF, Jul-Dec 63, III; memo, JOEG/V-ARPA Field Unit to C/S USAF, 3 Sep 63, subj: Eval of Test Results of Opl Test and Eval of U-10.

20. Memo, JOEG/V-ARPA Field Unit to C/S USAF, thru COMUSMAC/V and CINCPAC, 11 Oct 63, subj: 2d AD Test and Eval of TAPS in VN.

21. Final Rpt, Tac Anlys of T-28B A/C in RVN, 30 Apr 63, in Hist, 13th AF, Jul-Dec 63, II; Hist, 13th AF, Jul-Dec 63, pp 73-74; msg 97337, C/S USAF to PACAF, et al., 23 Nov 62.

22. Final Rpt, Tac Anlys of C-123B A/C in RVN, 15 Apr 63 and Tac Anlys of TF-102 A/C in RVN, 30 Jun 63, both in Hist, 13th AF, Jul-Dec 63, II; memo, Col R. B. Shick, Mil Asst to SAF, 14 Oct 63, subj: Tac Anlys of C-123B A/C in RVN, in OSAF 290-63.

23. Msg 96883, C/S USAF to PACAF, 18 Sep 63.

24. Memo, Burchinal to CINCPACAF, 26 Dec 63, no subj.

25. Memo, Dep SOD to Pres, 21 Nov 61, subj: Defol Ops in VN, 21 Nov 61; Rcrd, SOD Hono Conf, 16 Dec 61 and 15 Jan 62.

26. Memo, Brown to SA, et al., 29 Nov 61, subj: SVN; memo, P. F. Hilbert, Dep for Reqts Rev, Off of Under SAF, to Bundy, 12 Dec 61, no subj, in OSAF 1257-61; Rcrd, SOD Hono Conf, 16 Dec 61; memo, McKiernan to AFCHO, 3 May 65, in AFCHO.

27. Rcrd, SOD Hono Conf, 15 Jan 62, p 13, 59-60; Hist, PACAF, Jul-Dec 61, I, pt 2, p 28; Hist, 13th AF, Jul-Dec 61, p 86.

28. Rcrd, SOD Hono Conf, 15 Jan 62 and 19 Feb 62; Baltimore Sun, 25 Jan 62.

29. Memo, Col W. J. Meng, Exec, Vice C/S to SAF, 15 May 62, subj: Status of Defol Proj, SVN; ltr, CINCPAC to JCS, 24 Jul 62, no subj.

30. Ltr, Ch CHECO Team to J. W. Angell, Ch AFCHO, 3 Jun 63, subj: Hervicide Defol, in AFCHO; Hist, D/Ops, Jul-Dec 62, pp 43-44; NSA memo 178, 9 Aug 62, subj: Destruction of Mangrove Swamps in SVN; Rcrd, Discussions on VN at PACOM Hq, Dec 17-18, 1962, pp 41-43; JCS 2343/214, 21 Mar 62.

31. Memo, Chmn JCS to SOD, 28 Sep 62, subj: Rev and Opl Eval of Defol; memo, Chmn JCS to SOD, 9 Nov 62, subj: Defol Proj in SVN.

32. Memo, Dep SOD to Chmn JCS, 13 Oct 62, subj: Herbicide Proj; memo, Bundy to SOD, 27 Nov 62, subj: Defol/Herbicide Prog in SVN.

Notes to Pages 60 - 65   93

33. Rcrd, SOD Hono Conf, 23 Jul 62; LeMay Rpt, 24 Apr 62; memo, Chmn JCS to SOD, 28 Jul 62, subj: Chemical Crop Destruction, SVN; SOD to Pres, 8 Aug 62, same subj; memo, McBride to C/S USAF, 11 Sep 62, same subj; memo, Secy State to SOD, 28 Aug 62, subj: VN Proj for Crop Destruction.

34. Rcrd, SOD Hono Conf, 8 Oct 62; Hist, CINCPAC, 1962, pp 185-87; Hist, CINCPAC, 1963, p 227; Hist, D/Ops, 1 Jul-31 Dec 62, p 44; ltr, CINCPAC to JCS, 22 Mar 63, subj: Rpt Concerning Psych Aspects of Use of Defol in RVN; ltr, CHECO Team to Angell, 3 Jun 63.

35. Memo, Chmn JCS to SOD, 17 Apr 63, subj: Defol and Crop Destruction in SVN; Hist, D/Plans, Jan-Jun 63, p 238.

36. Hist, CINCPAC, 1963, pp 227-30; Hist, 13th AF, Jul-Dec 63, pp 68-69.

CHAPTER VII

1. Memo, L/Col N. F. Lambertson, Off D/Ops, to Dep D/Plans, 20 Jul 61, subj: Increase in GVN Border Patrol and Insurgency Suppression Capabilities; memo, Burchinal to C/S USAF, 20 Jun 61, subj: Increase in GVN Forces.

2. Memo for Rcrd by Off, COMUSMAC/V, 29 Sep 61, subj: Mtg at Independence Palace, Saigon; JCS 2343/27, 19 Oct 61.

3. JCS 2343/29, 25 Oct 61; memo, Burchinal to C/S USAF, 26 Oct 61, subj: SEA; memo, C/S USAF to JCS, 27 Oct 61, subj: SEA.

4. Memo for Rcrd by Off, COMUSMAC/V, 29 Sep 61; Rcrd, SOD Hono Conf, 16 Dec 61, item 7; Proj CHECO SEA Rpt, pt IV, pp 33-38.

5. Journal of Military Assistance (JMA), prep by Asst for Mutual Security, Sep 61, p 153; Dec 61, p 144; Jun 62, p 179; memo, Jt Staff to Chmn JCS, 14 Nov 61, subj: SVN; memo, Brown to SA, et al., 29 Nov 61, subj: SVN; Rcrd, SOD Hono Conf, 15 Jan 62; Hist, CINCPAC, 1962, p 190; Hist, 13th AF, 1962, pp 103-04; Hist, 2d ADVON, 15 Nov 61-8 Oct 62, app D, item 21; Air Force and Space Digest, Sep 64, p 103.

6. Rcrd, SOD Hono Conf, 21 Mar 62 and 23 Jul 62; Hist, 13th AF, 1962, pp 103-04; rpt, AF Study Gp on VN, May 1964, pt III.

7. LeMay Rpt, 24 Apr 62; Hist, CINCPAC, 1962, p 190.

8. Msg 36142, PACAF to C/S USAF, 18 Jan 63; ltr, CINCPAC to JCS, 25 Jan 63, subj: Comprehensive Plan for SVN; JCS 2343/203, 4 Mar 63; msg 36681, PACAF to C/S USAF, 2d ADVON, 13th AF, 16 Aug 62; Disosway Rpt, 22 Dec 62; Talking Paper for Chmn JCS for SOD Mtg, 25 Mar 63; no subj, 25 Mar 63; Hist, CINCPAC, 1963, pp 204-05.

9. Study, Sit in SVN, 17 Dec 62; msg 22419, PACAF to C/S USAF, 22 Feb 63; msg 33847, CINCPAC to Hq USAF, 15 Apr 63; memo, Dep SOD to Chmn JCS, 31 Dec 62, subj: Farmgate Aug, in OSAF 11-62; msg 160406, CINCPAC to JCS, 16 Apr 63, in Proj CHECO SEA Rpt, pt VI-B, doc 25; Hildreth, Special Air Warfare, 1963, pp 34-35.

10. Hildreth, Special Air Warfare, 1963, pp 34-35; Rcrd, SOD Hono Conf, 6 May 63; app 6; JMA, Dec 63, p 179.

11. JMA, Jun 63, p 193; Sep 63, p 187; Hildreth, Special Air Warfare, 1963, pp 34-35; Proj CHECO SEA Rpt, pt VI, p 28.

12. JMA, Sep 6, p 163.

13. Memo, L/G J. A. Dabney, Actg Asst SOD/ISA to Chmn JCS, 19 Aug 61, no subj; JCS 2343/22, 7 Oct 61; msg 33743, Dept of State-DOD to AmEmb Saigon, 19 Oct 61; JCS 2343/186, 15 Jan 63.

14. Rcrd, SOD Hono Conf, 23 Jul 61, pp 1-5; JCS 2343/186, 15 Jan 63; Disosway Rpt, 22 Dec 62; Proj CHECO SEA Rpt, pt III, pp 20-21.

15. JCS 2343/186, 15 Jan 63; ltr, SAF to SOD, 16 Mar 63, no subj.

16. Memo, B/G A. N. Williams, Dep D/Plans for Policy to Cold War Div, D/Plans, 15 Feb 63, subj: Geneva Agreements and Jets; msg 92474, C/S USAF to PACAF, 11 Apr 63.

17. Memo, SOD to Chmn JCS, 17 May 63, subj: Jet A/C for SVN; memo, SOD to SAF, 27 May 63, subj: A/C and Pilots for VNAF; Rcrd, SOD Hono Conf, 6 May 63; Proj CHECO SEA Rpt, pt III, p 22.

18. Msg 25890, PACAF to C/S USAF, 8 Jan 64; Proj CHECO SEA Rpt, pt III, p 22.

CHAPTER VIII

1. Msg 062345, COMUSMAC/V to JCS, et al., 6 Dec 62; msg COMUSMAC/V to JCS, et al., 10 Jan 63; New York Times, 18 Oct 64.

2. Christian Science Monitor, 20 Sep 62; New York Herald Tribune, 20 Sep 62; Washington Star, 8 Oct 62; New York Times, 13 Dec 62; Baltimore Sun, 21 Jan and 5 Feb 63; Washington Post, 2 Feb 63; Transcripts of SOD Press Confs, 23 and 30 Jan 63, in SAFOI; Senate Hearings before Cmte on Appropriations, 87th Cong, Foreign Assistance and Related Agencies Appropriations for 1963, p 771.

3. Memo, Worden to Cold War Div, D/Plans, 17 Dec 62, subj: Sit in SVN: An Appraisal; memo, Pancake to C/S USAF, 5 Jan 63, subj: Review of Mil Sit in SVN; SAF Press Statements, 8 Jan, 23 Feb 63, in SAFOI; Rcrd, SOD Hono Conf, 6 May 63, pp 1-a-8 to 1-a-9; Study, VC Infiltration, prep by Hq USMAC/V, 31 Oct 64.

Notes to Pages 70 - 75   95

4. Memo, Worden to Cold War Div, D/Plans, 17 Dec 62, subj: Sit in SVN.

5. Memo, Pancake to C/S USAF, 5 Jan 63, subj: Review of Mil Sit in SVN.

6. Ltr CINCPAC to Asst SOD/PA, 26 Nov 62, subj: News Correspondents View Concerning SVN War and Govt.

7. Rpt, by Sen Mike Mansfield, et al., to Senate Cmte on Foreign Relations, 88th Cong, 1st Sess, Vietnam and Southeast Asia, 1963, pp 6-8.

8. JCS 2343/221, 29 Mar 63; msg 56517, CINCPAC to JCS, 30 Apr 63; JCS 2343/241-1, 9 May 63; memo, Chmn JCS to SOD, 28 May 63; JCS 2343/248, 18 May 63; Rcrd, SOD Hono Conf, 6 May 63, pp 1-1 to 1-4; Hist, CINCPAC, 1963, pp 240-41.

9. Msg 19665, PACAF to C/S USAF, 5 Apr 63; Rcrd, SOD Hono Conf, 6 May 63, pp 4-a-1 to 4-a-3; Proj CHECO SEA Rpt, pt III, pp 45-49, and pt III-A, doc 49.

10. Rcrd, SOD Hono Conf, 6 May 63, pp 1-1 to 1-4; New York Times, 9 and 10 May 63; New York Times, 12 Jun 26 Aug, 10 Sep, and 17 Sep 63; Washington Post, 31 Oct 63.

11. Memo, Worden to C/S USAF, 27 Aug 63, subj: Background Paper on Pol Sit in SVN; New York Times, 3 Sep 63; Washington Post, 17 Sep 63; msg 38307, PACAF to C/S USAF, 29 Aug 63; House Hearings before Subcmte on Appropriations, 88th Cong, 2d Sess, DOD Appropriations for 1965, pt 4, p 11.

12. Memo, Chmn JCS to Pres, 9 Sep 63, subj: draft ltr, SOD to Secy State, 4 Nov 63; Senate Hearings before Subcmte on DOD Appropriations, 88th Cong, 2d Sess, DOD Appropriations for 1965, pt 1, pp 14-15; New York Times, 3 Oct 63.

13. New York Times, 3 Nov 63; Washington Post, 11 Nov 63; JMS, Dec 63, p 177.

14. Rcrd, SOD Hono Conf, 6 May 63; memo, Chmn JCS to SOD, 20 Aug 63, subj: Summary Rpt on 8th SOD Conf, 7 May 63; msg 4992, PACAF to C/S USAF, 3 Aug 63; Washington Post, 15, 16 Nov and 3 Dec 63; New York Times, 15 and 23 Dec 63.

15. NSA memo 273, 26 Nov 63; memo, SOD to SA, et al., 6 Dec 63, subj: NSA Memo 273, 26 Nov 63.

16. Memo, Pres to Chmn JCS, 2 Dec 63; msg 50231, CINCPAC to JCS, 26 Jan 64; New York Times, 21, 22 Dec 63 and 2 Jan 64.

17. Memo, C/S USAF to PACAF, 3 Dec 63; msg 85559, C/S USAF to PACAF, 17 Jan 64; memo, C/S USAF to JCS, 22 Jan 64, subj: Increase in Aerial Recon Capability in SEA; memo, JCS to SOD, 22 Jan 64, subj: VN and SEA; House Hearings before Subcmte on Appropriations, 88th Cong, 2d Sess, DOD Appropriations for 1965, pt 4, p 12.

GLOSSARY

ACTIV	Army Concepts Testing in Vietnam
AC&W	Aircraft Control and Warning
AFLC	Air Force Logistics Command
AFTU-V	Air Force Test Unit, Vietnam
ALO	Air Liaison Officer
AOC	Air Operations Center
App	Appendix
ARPA	Advanced Research Projects Agency
ARVN	Army of the Republic of Vietnam
ASOC	Air Support Operations Center
CDTC	Combat Test and Development Center
CHECO	Contemporary Historical Evaluation of Counterinsurgency Operations
C-E	Communications-Electronics
CIDG	Civilian Irregular Defense Group
CINCPAC	Commander-in-Chief, Pacific
CNO	Chief of Naval Operations
COIN	Counterinsurgency
CRC	Combat Reporting Center
CRP	Combat Reporting Post
DAF	Department of the Air Force
DCS/M	Deputy Chief of Staff, Materiel
DCS/P&O	Deputy Chief of Staff, Plans and Operations
DCS/P&P	Deputy Chief of Staff, Plans and Programs
DCS/S&L	Deputy Chief of Staff, Systems and Logistics
DDR&E	Director of Defense Research and Engineering
Defol	Defoliation
D/Ops	Directorate of Operations
FAC	Forward Air Controller
HONO	Honolulu
HSAS	Headquarters Support Activity, Saigon
ICC	International Control Commission
JAOC	Joint Air Operations Center
JCS	Joint Chiefs of Staff
JMA	Journal of Military Assistance
JMS	Journal of Mutual Security
JOEG/V	Joint Operational Evaluations Group, Vietnam
MAAG/V	Military Assistance Advisory Group, Vietnam
MAC/V	Military Assistance Command, Vietnam
MAP	Military Assistance Program

NCP	National Campaign Plan
NSAM	National Security Action Memorandum
NSC	National Security Council
NVN	North Vietnam
OSAF	Office of the Secretary of the Air Force
OSD	Office of the Secretary of Defense
OSD/ISA	Office of the Secretary of Defense, International Security Affairs
PACAF	Pacific Air Force
PACOM	Pacific Command
PCS	Permanent Change of Station
PPC	Photo Processing Cell
Prog	Program
Proj	Project
RVNAF	Republic of Vietnam Armed Forces
SAF	Secretary of the Air Force
SAFOI	Secretary of the Air Force Office of Information
SAW	Special Air Warfare
SEA	Southeast Asia
SEATO	Southeast Asia Treaty Organization
Sit	Situation
SOD	Secretary of Defense
Strat	Strategic
SVN	South Vietnam
TACS	Tactical Air Control System
TAPS	Tactical Air Positioning System
USAR	U.S. Army
USARPAC	U.S. Army, Pacific
USARSG/V	U.S. Army Special Group, Vietnam
USMAAG/V	U.S. Military Assistance Advisory Group, Vietnam
USMAC/V	U.S. Military Assistance Command, Vietnam
VN	Vietnam
VNAF	Republic of Vietnam Air Force

APPENDICES: STATISTICS ON SOUTH VIETNAM

APPENDIX 1

Farmgate Combat Training Sorties

Operational	1962*			1963			Grand Total
	B-26	T-28	Total	B-26	T-28	Total	
Close Air Support	150	446	596	660	1,077	1,737	2,333
Interdiction	334	346	680	1,432	1,383	2,815	3,495
Escort Helicopter	21	359	380	98	450	548	928
Escort Aircraft	21	69	90	137	307	444	534
Escort Convoy	30	16	46	91	48	139	185
Escort Train	--	14	14	--	35	35	49
Air Cover	67	129	196	410	501	911	1,107
Armed Reconnaissance	31	282	313	52	724	776	1,089
Photo Reconnaissance	429	121	550	523	11	534	1,084
Visual Reconnaissance	9	20	29	62	272	334	363
Defensive	9	10	19	164	--	164	183
Other	39	41	80	45	40	85	165
Total	1,140	1,853	2,993	3,674	4,848	8,522	11,515
Nonoperational							
(Administrative, deployment, test, etc.)	479	967	1,446	299	573	872	2,318
Flying Time (Hours)	3,953	4,505	8,458	9,494	8,554	18,048	26,506

*Includes Dec 1961 in these appendices where applicable.

SOURCE: Data Control Br, Sys Div, Dir of Ops, DCS/P&O.

APPENDIX 2

Results of Farmgate Missions

	1962	1963	Total
Enemy Killed	3,200	3,256	6,456
Enemy Wounded	--	556*	556
Structures Destroyed	4,000	5,750	9,750
Structures Damaged	--	6,253*	6,253
Boats Destroyed	275	2,643	2,918
Boats Damaged	--	302*	302

*Includes figures for 1962.

APPENDIX 3

USAF U-10 and TO-1D Sorties

Type Aircraft	1962	1963	Total
U-10	351*	2,404	2,755
TO-1D	--	3,957+	3,957

*Began operational flights in Sep 1962.

+Began operational flights in Jul 1963.

SOURCE: Memo, M/G R.F. Worden to C/S USAF, 23 Jan 64, subj: JCS Briefing by Gen. Anthis.

APPENDIX 4

USAF C-123 and SC-47 Sorties and Logistic Activities

C-123 Operations

	1962	1963	Total
Sorties	11,689	24,429	36,118
Passengers	54,734	142,124	196,858
Troops Airlanded	32,906	1,349	34,255
Training Troops Dropped	8,952	2,072	11,024
Combat Landing Team Troops Dropped	3,501	--	3,501
Combat Troops Air Evacuation	--	47	47
Cargo Airborne Resupply (Tons)	1,973.1	613.5	2,586.6
Cargo Airlifted (Tons)	15,346.5	32,396	47,742.5
Flying Time (Hours)	17,842	29,255	47,097

SC-47 Sorties

Operational	1962	1963	Total
Reconnaissance	12	--	12
Flare Drop	21	51	72
Airborne Alert	--	5	5
Paradrops	1	293	294
Special Forces Support	649	2,578	3,227
Radio Relay	4	5	9
Other	147	42	189
Total	834	2,974	3,808

Nonoperational

	1962	1963	Total
(Administrative, training, test, etc.)	1,376	1,428	2,804
Flying Time (Hours)	.836	5,289	8,125

SOURCE: Data Control Br, Sys Div, Dir of Ops, DCS/P&O.

APPENDIX 5

VNAF A-1H and T-28 Sorties

	1962			1963			Grand
	A-1H	T-28	Total	A-1H	T-28	Total	Total
Operational							
Interdiction	969	1,379	2,348	1,605	3,331	4,936	7,284
Air Support	--	234	234	500	493	993	1,227
Escort Helicopter	80	407	487	116	374	490	977
Escort Convoy	93	36	129	74	106	180	309
Escort Aircraft	26	51	77	116	387	503	580
Escort Train	27	52	79	520	278	798	877
Air Cover	384	211	595	790	443	1,233	1,828
Armed Reconnaissance	26	144	170	154	1,099	1,253	1,423
Visual Reconnaissance	--	--	--	--	24	24	24
Air Defense	12	--	12	6	48	54	66
Other	257	108	365	49	148	197	562
Total	1,874	2,622	4,496	3,930	6,731	10,661	15,157
Nonoperational							
(Training, test, deployment, etc.)	1,204	3,730	4,934	1,263	3,717	4,980	9,914
Flying Time (Hours)	7,179	7,778	14,957	9,914	12,757	22,671	37,628

SOURCE: Data Control Br, Sys Div, Dir of Ops, DCS/P&O.

APPENDIX 6

U.S. and VNAF Military Aircraft

	1961*	1962*	1963*
USAF	35	63	117
VNAF	152	180	228
U.S. Army	40+	200	325
U.S. Marine Corps	--	20	20
Total	227	463	690

*As of December each year.

+Approximate.

SOURCE: Project CHECO Southeast Asia Report, Oct 61-Dec 63, pt 1, chart 1-2; Office, Asst for Mutual Security, DCS/S&L.

APPENDIX 7

U.S. Aircraft Lost, 1 Jan 1962-31 Mar 1964

	Fixed Wing	Rotary	Total
USAF	34	--*	34
U.S. Army	16	54	70
U.S. Marine Corps	--*	10	10
Total	40	64	114

*No USAF or Marine aircraft of these types.

SOURCE: Rpt of Air Force Study Gp on VN, May 1964, in OSAF.

APPENDIX 8

USAF Aircraft Destroyed and Damaged

	1962			1963		
	Destroyed by Enemy	Destroyed Other Causes	Damaged*	Destroyed by Enemy	Destroyed Other Causes	Damaged
B-26	1	0	–	3	3	60
C-123	1	3	–	0	3	66
C-47	1	1	–	0	0	10
T-28	2	0	–	2	2	72
T0-1D	0	0	–	1	1	13
U-3	0	0	–	0	1	0
U-10	1	0	–	0	0	8
Total	6	4		6	10	229

*No records available for 1962.

SOURCE: Memo, M/G R. F. Worden, Dep Dir of Plans, DCS/P&O to C/S USAF, 16 Apr 64, subj: Addit A/C (A-1E's) for RVN, in Plans RL (64) 38-9.

APPENDIX 9

U.S. Military Personnel

	Dec 61	Jul 62	Dec 62	Mar 63	Sep 63	Dec 63
Army		6,155	7,885	8,718	10,795	10,119
Air Force	421*	1,699	2,422	3,256	4,444	4,630
Navy		320	447	585	668	757
Marines		648	535	584	551	483
Total		8,822	11,289	13,143	16,458	15,989

*Excluding Air Force Section MAAG/V.

SOURCE: Stat Rpt, Trends in Counterinsurgency, 21 Sep 63; msg 271045, 2d AD to PACAF, 27 Apr 64.

APPENDIX 10

Combat Casualties

U.S., Vietnamese, and Viet Cong Battle Casualties*

	1961	1962	1963	Total
South Vietnam	9,000	13,000	19,000	41,000
Viet Cong	13,000	33,000	28,000	74,000
United States	--	101	491	592
Total	22,000	46,101	47,491	115,592

U.S. Casualties by Type*

	1962**	1963	Total
Killed in Action	21	72	93
Wounded in Action	80	406	486
Missing in Action	0	13	13
Non-battle Deaths	34	37	71
Non-battle Injuries	45	73	118
Total	180	601	781

USAF Combat Casualties, Dec 1961-Dec 1963+

Killed in Action	27
Wounded in Action	22
Missing in Action	4
Total	53

---

*SOURCE: Hist of 13 AF, Jul-Dec 63, p 53.

**Includes Dec 1961.

+SOURCE: Rpt of AF Study Gp in VN, May 1964, in OSAF.

www.ingramcontent.com/pod-product-compliance
Lightning Source LLC
Chambersburg PA
CBHW080442170426
43195CB00017B/2863